Decoding Git Guidebook for Developers

Learn How Git's Code Works

Jacob Stopak, Initial Commit LLC

Also by Initial Commit LLC:

Coding Essentials Guidebook for Developers

Visit https://initialcommit.com/store for details.

Decoding Git Guidebook for Developers by Jacob Stopak
Published by Initial Commit LLC
initialcommit.com

ISBN: 978-1-959595-00-7

FIRST EDITION

Note from the author

This guidebook heavily references Git's original code as updated and maintained by the Baby-Git project – also created by Jacob Stopak, Initial Commit LLC – which can be found at the following link:

https://bitbucket.org/jacobstopak/baby-git/src/master/README.md

The Baby-Git project contains Git's original source code, reorganized and thoroughly commented for the reader's optimal learning experience. The authors of this guidebook highly suggest perusing the link above, downloading the accompanying Baby-Git source code, and looking through the code/comments with your own eyes to really get a feel for how the code is laid out. This Decoding Git Guidebook for Developers is meant to accompany the tools provided at the link above in order to help curious developers understand how Git's code actually works.

A tar archive of the latest version of the Baby-Git source code can be downloaded from the following link:

https://initialcommit.com/baby-git-tar

Table of Contents

Part 1: Git's Initial Commit - General User Guide

In the first part of this guidebook, we will provide a detailed discussion of the concepts and components that comprise Git's original repository, instructions for installing the original Git program, and a tutorial for using the 7 original Git commands that make up the program.

1 Introduction

1.1 Structure of a Software Project

Git is a tool that is widely used by software development teams to track and manage changes in software projects as they evolve over time. The term **software project** may sound intimidating and vague, but really it is very simple. As illustrated in Figure 1.1 below, a software project is nothing more than a set of files and folders containing code.

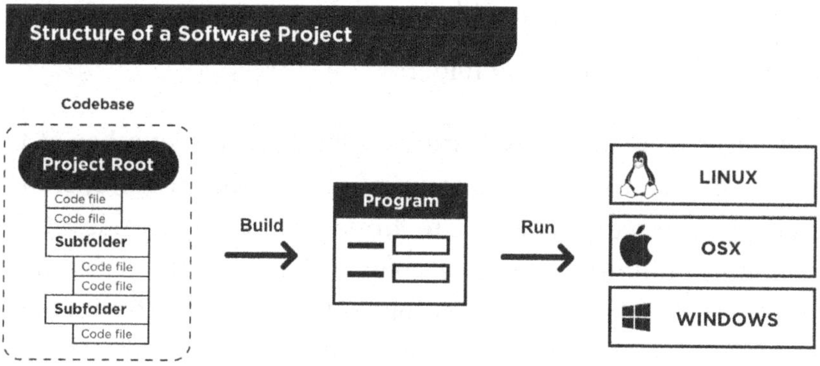

Figure 1.1: Structure of a Software Project

The full set directories and files that make up a software project is called a codebase. The **Project Root** is the highest-level folder in the project's directory tree. Code files can be included directly in the project root or organized into multiple levels of folders.

As specified in the second step of Figure 1.1, when the codebase is ready for testing or deployment it can be **built** into the program that will actually run on your computer. The **build** process can include one or more steps that convert the code written by humans into a form that is understandable by your computer's processing chips. Once the code is built, your program is ready to run on your specific operating system, such as Linux, OSX, or

Windows.

1.2 Collaborative Development Efforts

Over time, developers update the project code to add new features, fix bugs, implement security updates, and more. In general, there are three ways developers can make these changes to a software project:

1. Add new files and folders to the project
2. Edit the code in existing files and folders
3. Delete existing files and folders

As projects grow and new features are added, the number of files and folders (as well as the amount of code within them) increases. Large projects can grow up to hundreds of thousands of files containing millions of lines of code. To support this growth, the number of developers on large project teams typically increases. Large software projects can have hundreds or even thousands of developers all working in tandem.

This begs the question: "How the heck do all these developers, who may be geographically spread out all around the world, keep track of their software project code in such a way that they can work together on a single project?" Development teams need a way to keep track of exactly what changes were made to the code, which files or folders were affected, who made each change, and need a way for each developer to be able to obtain the updates from all other developers. Figure 1.2 illustrates a simplified development scenario with 3 team members, Mat, Jack, and Karina. Git provides a way to accomplish all of this and more. Tools that provide this ability are called Version Control Systems, or VCS for short.

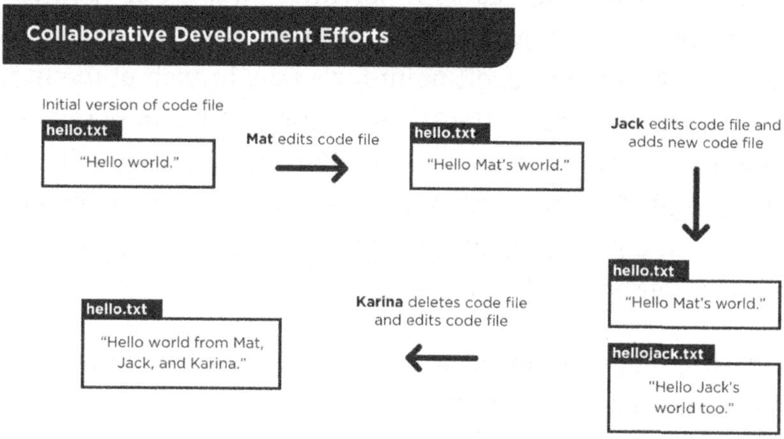

Figure 1.2: Collaborative Development Efforts

Git is versatile and not limited to the field of software development. It can be used to accurately track changes in most digital files and provides a convenient means for keeping a history of those changes. A group of scientists, for example, could use Git to write a scientific paper collaboratively. The edits made to the Word document draft of this guidebook as it is being written are tracked through Git as well.

VCS systems like Git are tools that enable a user to take a snapshot of the state of a project at chosen times, whether it is a project that consists of a single file or a larger project consisting of a cascade of directories. Perhaps more accurately, the snapshot that is recorded is the set of changes made to the project since the previous snapshot. In VCS jargon, the user commits the changes to a repository of those changes.

It is easy to think of ways that such a means for accurately knowing the state of a project at particular points in the past could be useful to the project. Besides record keeping and providing a potential backup source, such a system, for example, enables one to fix mistakes in the current state of a project by reverting the project to a previously working state.

Each snapshot also serves as a potential jumping-off point for a new line of project development. In other words, each snapshot could serve as a jumping-off point for a new branch of the project. The accurate tracking of the state of a project made possible by a versioning system also makes possible collaboration, in which multiple contributors could simultaneously make their respective changes to the project, changes which they could later merge into a coherent version of the project.

The basic functionalities of a VCS like Git can be summarized as providing a user the ability to:

- Add project files and folders to a repository
- Commit changes made to the files to the repository at user-chosen times, i.e. save snapshots of the project
- Access the history of the changes committed to the repository
- See the differences in the state of the project at different commit times
- Branch from a particular committed version
- Merge changes from different branches

1.3 Origins of Git

Created by Linus Torvalds (the creator of Linux) in 2005, Git has evolved over more than a decade to become the sophisticated, convenient, and ubiquitous tool that it is today. This guidebook, however, is about the precursor to this evolved version of Git. It is about a set of commands that were, in the parlance of versioning, the Initial Commit of the Git application.

Git's initial commit could be thought of as a first rudimentary version of Git. Although much less sophisticated and convenient than its grown-up version. Nevertheless, it encapsulates the core ideas behind modern-day Git. Figure 1.3 illustrates the origins of

Git. Moreover, a primary motivation behind Git was to be efficient in implementing these repository functionalities, and it did so by implementing data deflation (more commonly known as compression) and the use of a cryptographic hash function called SHA-1 to map data to hash values or message digests. This combination of data deflation and hashing is the central concept that underlies the algorithms used in Git.

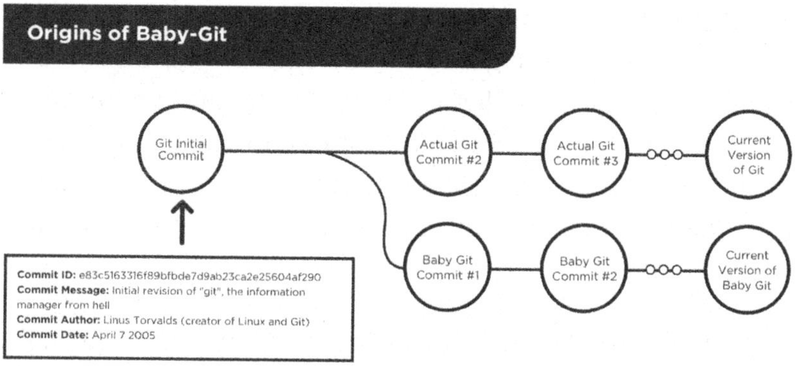

Figure 1.3: Origins of Git

Git's initial commit is written in the C programming language and consists of about 1,000 lines of code and a total of 7 commands, and they actually work. The simplicity and "smallness" of the code make Git's initial commit the perfect codebase for curious developers to study in order to learn how the code works. The fact that arguably the most popular and important tool for collaborative software development in the history of the coding world is simple enough for a novice developer to understand directly from its initial code is really an amazing thing.

1.4 Goal of this book

The goals of this guidebook are twofold:

1. It aims to introduce the reader to the concepts and components behind Git's original repository and commands, and to provide

a tutorial of how these commands are used in practice.

2. It aims to use Git's initial commit as a tool for exploring the underpinnings of the Git versioning system. By exploring the concepts and implementation behind this rudimentary program, it is hoped that the reader will gain insights into how a much larger application like Git is programmed at conception.

This guidebook is divided roughly along these lines into two parts. Part 1 is a general user guide to Git's initial commit, comprising Chapters 1 through 4. In Chapter 2, we discuss the general concepts and components of Git's initial commit. In Chapter 3, we provide a guide for installing Git's original first version in a local machine. And in Chapter 4, we provide a tutorial for using the 7 original Git commands.

Part 2 of this guidebook, consisting of Chapters 5 through 13, delves into the actual code of Git's initial commit. Each of the 7 original Git commands is discussed in detail in its own chapter and we look under the hood at the more salient parts of the command's underlying C code.

This guidebook is targeting readers who have some experience using the Git application and who are interested in knowing more about its origins, underlying concepts, and how it is implemented at the code level. Some programming experience would be an advantage but not necessary. Readers with no programming experience, for example, might be more interested in Part 1 of this guidebook. These are, of course, not requirements of the reader, and an innate curiosity about how things work might be sufficient reason for perusing this guidebook.

The reader can download the package that accompanies this guidebook from this link:

https://initialcommit.com/baby-git-tar

Instructions for compiling and installing this package are given in Chapter 3.

1.5 Resources

The following links are C language resources that served as references when this guidebook was being written and which the reader could consult as well:

The GNU C library:
https://www.gnu.org/software/libc/manual/html_node/index.html

The IEEE POSIX standards:
http://pubs.opengroup.org/onlinepubs/9699919799/
(Use the search box to search for C functions).

A C and C++ reference:
http://www.cplusplus.com/reference/
(Use the search box to search for C functions).

The zlib manual:
https://zlib.net/manual.html

A zlib usage example:
https://zlib.net/zlib_how.html

2 An Overview of Git's Initial Commit

As mentioned in Chapter 1, Git's initial commit is a rudimentary version of the modern Git version control application that is widely used today. The original program is written in the C language and has a total of 7 commands that are run on the command line.

NOTE	Git's current codebase (as of 2022) is still written mostly in C. However, it does make use of a few other languages for certain features, including shell scripts, Perl, Tcl, and Python.

Git's initial commit enables a user to set up a local repository to which the user can add files to be tracked and subsequently update the repository when changes are made to those files. Other functionalities include the ability to list the files that have been committed to the repository, to display the contents of those files, and to show the differences between the cached snapshots of the files and the working versions of those files.

As stated in Git's original README file, Git was designed as an efficient directory management system. The key to achieving this goal was to make use of file deflation (compression) in combination with a hash function, specifically the SHA-1 hash function, to map arbitrary file contents to unique hash values. Figure 2.1 illustrates a high-level overview of the data compression and decompression process that Git makes use of.

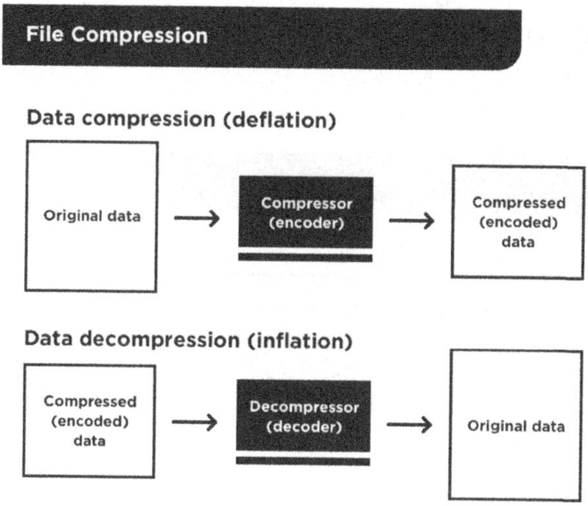

Figure 2.1: File Compression

The **Original data** box represents the code files in a software project. When Git is told to track a new file or register file modifications, the content in these files are read into memory and compressed to a size that makes them more efficient to store and transfer over a network. Every version of a tracked file is stored as a **loose object** in the local repository - Git's 3 original types of loose objects will be covered in the next section. When the data in a loose object is retrieved for use, it is decompressed to yield the original contents.

Let us now move on to hash functions. A hash function is a one-way function – a function that case be easily run in one direction to convert an input to an output, but cannot easily be reversed to convert the output value back into the input. In addition, each input to the hash function produces a unique output. Consider a file with the text "hello world" inside of it. We can take that text and pump it through the SHA-1 hash function to yield a unique output code. If we update the text to read "hello cruel world" and re-hash it, we will get a new unique hash output value since the content has changed. As we will see, all objects in Git are indexed and referenced through their respective SHA-1 hash values, which are also known as **object IDs**. Figure 2.2 illustrates how hash functions work.

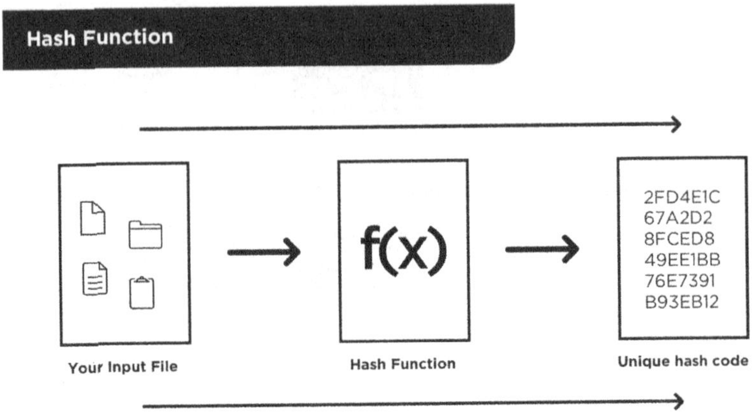

Figure 2.2: Hash Function

As an aside, hash functions are a core part of the HTTPS protocol that secures Internet traffic as well as cryptocurrency technologies like Bitcoin. In both of these use cases, there is an important need to compute a unique hash value of a secret **private key**, in which the hash value (output) becomes the **public key** - think Bitcoin public address or HTTPS certificate - which can be shared publicly.

In the case of SHA-1, a hash value has a length of 160 bits, or 20 bytes. Remember, a bit is just a "slot" in memory representing a binary (base-2) value of 0 or 1. A byte is a sequence of 8 bits, and is typically the smallest slice of memory available for modern processors to work with.

SHA-1 hash values are usually expressed in hexadecimal representation (base-16), using the digits 0123456789abcdef. This allows the SHA-1 hash value to be rendered as a sequence of 40 digits, which is more user-friendly than a 160-bit binary number or a decimal number. This means that Git's code contains functions for converting SHA-1 hash values from binary to hex and vice-versa.

Each 2-digit hexadecimal number has a range of possible values from 00 to FF, or 0 to 255 in decimal representation. Here is an example of a SHA-1 hash value in hexadecimal representation:

```
47a013e660d408619d894b20806b1d5086aab03b
```

NOTE To illustrate how the math works, each pair of digits in a hex SHA-1 like the one seen above can store a maximum value of FF (corresponding to 255 in decimal), and that requires 1 byte of storage since 11111111 in binary is 255 in decimal. Since 20 pairs of hex digits make up the whole 40-digit SHA-1, this equates to a total length of 20 bytes.

Since all objects in Git are indexed and referenced through their hash values, a hash rendered in this particular hexadecimal format is the basic naming unit that users of Git will be working with to manage their repository.

In general terms, an initial workflow for adding and committing files to a Git repository consists of the following steps:

1. Initialize the repository database.
2. Add files to the repository database and the corresponding metadata to the repository cache.
3. Write metadata in the cache to the repository database.
4. Commit the current changeset to the repository database.

When changes are subsequently made to the tracked files, the user can then update the repository database and cache with these new changes.

2.1 Components of a Git Repository

A repository in Git's initial commit has four basic components:

1. Objects
2. An object database
3. A current directory cache
4. A working directory

Each of these components will be discussed in turn.

Objects

An object is an abstraction of data and metadata. It is an arbitrary set of content – it could be text content in a file, or audio data, or any arbitrary byte stream – that is indexed and referenced through its hash value. In other words, the name of an object is its unique hash value, and this hash value is used to refer to and look up that specific piece of content. It is important to note that an object's hash value is the hash of the deflated (compressed) data and metadata represented by the object, not of the inflated data and metadata.

NOTE	In Git's current codebase as of 2022, the order of operations has been reversed and object are hashed before they are compressed. The benefit of this is that the calculated hash values (object IDs) are not dependent on the compression algorithm in use. This means the compression algorithm can effectively be swapped out while preserving the preexisting object IDs.

The general structure of an object is as follows:

```
object tag
' '                    (single space)
size of object data (in bytes)
'\0'                   (null character)
object binary data
```

NOTE In Git's code objects are formatted on a single line, but in the example above we put each part on a different line for visual understanding.

As you can see, the first part of an object consists of the object metadata, and the second part consists of the object data (object binary data). A single space and a null byte `\0` are used as delimiters between the elements.

The metadata consists of a string containing an object tag that indicates the object type and a string containing the size of the object data in bytes before deflation.

There are three types of objects in Git's initial commit: A blob object, a tree object, and a commit or changeset object. Thus, the object tag in the structure above can be **blob**, **tree**, or **commit**.

Blob object

A blob (Binary Large OBject) object is a general abstraction for user data. In practical use, this type of object contains the contents of a digital file that a user has added to the repository. In other words, a blob object is a type of object that corresponds to a user file in binary form – it could be any type of file the user wishes to add to the repository, such as a plaintext file, video file, Word document, etc. Git will generate a blob object for each file that a user adds to the repository, and this blob object will be named, indexed, and referenced through the deflated blob object's SHA-1 hash value.

A blob object has the following structure:

```
"blob"              (blob object tag)
' '                 (single space)
size of blob data (in bytes)
'\0'                (null character)
blob data
```

Tree object

A tree object contains a list of files that have been added by a user to the repository. A tree's purpose is to correlate file names and other file metadata with blobs representing the actual file content that has been added to the repository. As with any object, a tree object is named, indexed, and referenced through the deflated tree object's SHA-1 hash value.

A tree object has the following structure:

```
"tree"              (tree object tag)
' '                 (single space)
size of tree data (in bytes)
'\0'                (null character)
file 1 mode         (octal number)
' '
file 1 path
'\0'
blob 1 SHA-1 hash (hash of deflated blob)
file 2 mode
' '
file 2 path
'\0'
blob 2 SHA-1 hash
...
file N mode
' '
```

```
file N path
'\0'
blob N SHA-1 hash
```

In the structure above, file 1, file 2, etc. refer to files that the user has added to the repository. For each file, the mode, path/name, and SHA-1 hash of the corresponding blob object are stored in the tree object. The file mode is an octal number whose value gives the file permissions and type, as defined in Unix-like systems. The file path is just the regular path (including name) of the file. The SHA-1 hash is the hash value of the deflated blob object in the object database that corresponds to the file.

The file information is sorted lexicographically by file path. The size of the tree that's recorded in the tree object metadata is the sum of the sizes of the file information entries in the tree object data.

Commit object

A commit or changeset object is the result of committing a tree object to the repository database. It contains the hash value of the tree object being committed, the hash values of any parent tree objects specified by the user, metadata about the user who committed the tree, the time and date when the commit was made, and a user-supplied comment known today as the **commit message**.

By enabling a user to specify parent trees of the tree object being committed, a commit object makes possible keeping a history of the committed tree object. This means that even in Git's initial commit, primitive branching and merging were possible, although they required a manual, intensive effort to work with. Like any other object, a commit object is named, indexed, and referenced through the deflated commit object's SHA-1 hash value.

A commit object has the following structure:

```
"commit"               (commit object tag)
' '                    (single space)
size of commit data (in bytes)
'\0'                   (null character)
tree SHA-1 hash        (hash of root tree)
parent 1 SHA-1 hash (1st parent tree hash)
parent 2 SHA-1 hash (2nd parent tree hash)
...
author ID email date
committer ID email date
(empty line)
user comment
```

As usual, the hash values indicated above all refer to hash values of deflated objects. Note that it is possible to specify up to 16 parent tree objects in Git's initial commit.

The object database

Another component of a Git repository is the **object database**. This database is simply an organized set of folders and files used for locally storing blob, tree, and commit objects for use with Git.

The first step in setting up a Git repository is to initialize the object database. The user can specify an existing objects directory through an environment variable called `SHA1_FILE_DIRECTORY`. If not specified by the user, the program defaults to creating the directory `.dircache/objects` in the current folder to represent the object database directory.

Under the object database directory, the program creates 256 subfolders that are named from **00** to **ff**, corresponding to the 256 possible values of a two-digit hexadecimal number. In other words, the database directories will be as follows:

```
.dircache/objects/00
.dircache/objects/01
.dircache/objects/02
...
.dircache/objects/fd
.dircache/objects/fe
.dircache/objects/ff
```

When Git needs to store an object, it is stored under the directory whose name is the same as the first two digits of the object's SHA-1 hash value rendered in a 40-digit hexadecimal representation. The remaining 38 digits of an object's hash value in hexadecimal representation are then used as the base filename of that object. For example, an object (let's assume it's a blob object) with a hash value of:

```
47a013e660d408619d894b20806b1d5086aab03b
```

will have a path in the database that is equal to

```
.dircache/objects/47/a013e660d408619d894b20806b1d5086aab03b
```

Note how the first two characters of the hash value represent the name of the subfolder to store the object in, and the remaining characters of the hash value specify the file name. Thus, an object's hash value completely specifies the path and name of the object in the object database.

The current directory cache

The **current directory cache** is the equivalent of the modern day Git **staging area**, which is also known as Git's **index**. We tend to think of the staging area in a very conceptual way as Git users, but in reality it is just a plain old binary file stored at `.dircache/index`, that contains information, or metadata, about files that have been added by the user to the repository. When a user adds a file to the repository, the program adds a corresponding blob file to the object database, and the current directory cache is also updated to contain the file's metadata and the blob object's hash value.

NOTE	File information in the current directory cache is sorted **lexicographically** by file path. This just means that the so called cache entries are sorted in a generalized alphabetical order that takes into account numbers and symbols in addition to lowercase and uppercase letters.

All the information needed for creating a tree object is stored in the cache. The cache also holds additional file metadata that is not used in tree objects. The current directory cache can thus be thought of as an intermediate representation of a tree object, or as a **factory for building trees**.

File metadata and blob object hashes stored in the cache do not have to be consistent with the working versions of the corresponding user files. Edits and changes to the user files are not automatically reflected in the cache. However, the cache is used to provide an efficient way of obtaining any differences between the file information stored in it and the working versions of the files.

As mentioned, the current directory cache is stored in a file called `.dircache/index` in the user's current working directory and has the following structure:

```
cache header
cache entry 1
cache entry 2
cache entry 3
...
```

```
cache entry N
```

In this structure, cache entry 1, cache entry 2, etc. refer respectively to information about file 1, file 2, etc. Each cache entry stores the following information or metadata about a user file:

```
file's last status change time
file's last modification time
ID of device containing the file
file inode number
file mode (type and permissions)
file user ID
file group ID
file size in bytes
SHA-1 hash value of corresponding deflated blob object
file path length
file path
```

Note that several of these are file properties that are specific to Unix-like systems, namely the status change time, device ID, inode number, mode, user ID, and group ID.

The cache structure also contains a cache header, which consists of the following information:

```
signature (common to all cache headers)
program version number
number of cache entries, N, in the cache
SHA-1 hash value of the deflated cache entries
```

The information in the cache header is used by Git's code to verify the content entries in the index file.

Working directory

The **working directory** refers to the base user directory containing the user files that the user wants to track and add to the repository. Only files residing in this directory or below it can be added to the repository, and not all existing user files have to be added to the repository.

The working directory also contains the `.dircache/` directory created by the Git program to store the index file (current directory cache), as well as the objects directory (object database) if an existing object database was not specified by the user. The `.dircache` directory and its contents should not be edited by the user, except possibly for moving the object database to another directory.

User files and folders in the working directory and below it can be freely edited. The `.dircache/index` cache file in the working directory is used to determine if changes have been made to files in the working directory since those files were last added to or updated in the cache.

Figure 2.3 below illustrates the components of a repository in Git's initial commit.

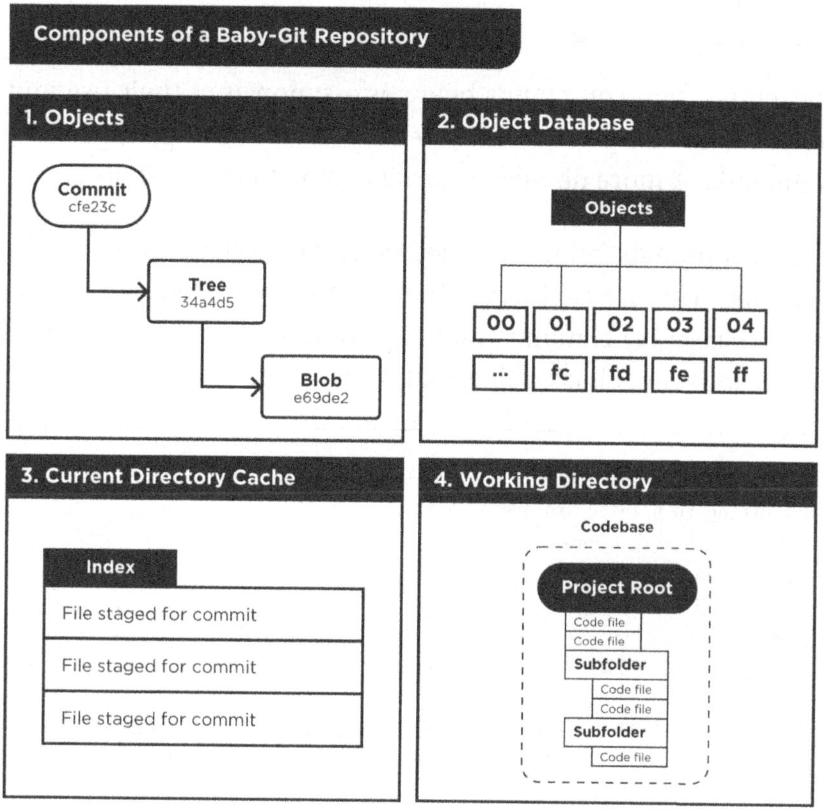

Figure 2.3: Components of a Git Repository

2.2 Synopsis of Git's Original Commands

The 7 original Git commands are:

```
init-db
update-cache
write-tree
commit-tree
read-tree
cat-file
```

```
show-diff
```

The sequence of commands below is a synopsis of their use and is shown here to provide the reader a general picture of the commands. A more detailed tutorial can be found in Chapter 4.

In the commands below, the files **hello.txt** and **changelog** are both user files. The file **hello.txt** contains the text "Hello world!" and the file **changelog** contains the text "Initial commit.". Notice the 40-digit hexadecimal hash values output by some of the commands.

```
$ init-db
defaulting to private storage area

$ update-cache hello.txt

$ write-tree
60471dd2f6a67990755795708b2a09a5b3da505c

$ commit-tree 60471dd2f6a67990755795708b2a09a5b3da505c < changelog
Committing initial tree 60471dd... deae7e7a5111831cd90e4f10379d798e135f734a

$ cat-file deae7e7a5111831cd90e4f10379d798e135f734a
temp_git_file_LarhKM: commit

$ cat temp_git_file_LarhKM
tree 60471dd2f6a67990755795708b2a09a5b3da505c
author Crusoe,,, <rcrusoe@island> Fri Apr 27 13:41:01 2018
committer Crusoe,,, <rcrusoe@island> Fri Apr 27 13:41:01 2018
Initial commit.

$ read-tree 60471dd2f6a67990755795708b2a09a5b3da505c
100664 hello.txt (694cdbbdce662aa1060d07cba1d4e0cfeb822bee)

$ cat-file 694cdbbdce662aa1060d07cba1d4e0cfeb822bee
temp_git_file_kEtFzM: blob

$ cat temp_git_file_kEtFzM
Hello world!

$ show-diff
hello.txt: ok
```

3 Installing Git's Original Version

This chapter is a guide for installing the original Git program. In this case, installing means downloading the Git's original package, compiling the C source code, and then copying the Git executables to a user-defined command path.

Originally, the code was intended to be compiled and run in Unix-like environments, but for the purpose of this guidebook it has also been adapted to compile and run under Windows in a MinGW-w64 and MSYS2 environment. For Windows users, there is a guide in the Appendix for installing MSYS2 and MinGW-w64 in Windows. Under this environment, the procedure for installing and compiling the code is the same as that given below (see section 3.2, "Installation steps").

We tested compiling Git's original codebase in the following environments: Ubuntu 16.04, Debian 9.4, CentOS 7.4, Fedora 27, FreeBSD 11.1, macOS 10.13.x High Sierra and in Windows 7 using the MinGW-w64 and MSYS2 environment. In general, the user should be able to compile and run the code in other Unix-like environments.

3.1 System requirements

The following tools and libraries are required to compile Git's original codebase.

Tools for building a C program

A C **compiler** and the GNU version of the **make** command are needed to compile the C code supplied with this guidebook. These are typically included in a system's C development package. You can use the following commands to check if a C compiler and GNU `make` are installed in your system.

For Linux systems (including MSYS2 in Windows) and macOS:

```
$ cc --version
$ make --version
```

For FreeBSD:

```
$ cc --version
$ gmake --version
```

If the above commands output version numbers, then the required build tools are installed in your system. Otherwise, you need to install a C development package in your system. The commands for installing a C development package are given below for some systems.

In Debian systems (Ubuntu, Mint, etc.):

```
$ sudo apt-get update
$ sudo apt-get install build-essential
```

In RHEL systems (Fedora, CentOS, etc.):

```
$ sudo dnf update
$ sudo dnf groupinstall "c development tools and libraries"
```

In Arch Linux systems (including MSYS2 in Windows):

```
$ pacman -Syu
```

```
$ pacman -S --needed base-devel
```

A FreeBSD system will probably come with clang as its default C compiler. The code will compile with this compiler. However, the GNU version of the **make** command is needed in order to use the **Makefile** supplied with Git's original code.

NOTE A Makefile is a plaintext file that tells the C compiler toolchain how to build (compile and link) the program.

In FreeBSD, the corresponding command is **gmake**. Use the following command to install gmake:

```
$ sudo pkg install gmake
```

zlib development library

In order to deflate and inflate data, the Git uses the **zlib development library**. Here are the commands for installing this library in some systems. This library is likely already installed in macOS and no action needs to be taken.

In Debian systems (Ubuntu, Mint, etc.):

```
$ sudo apt-get update
$ sudo apt-get install zlib1g-dev
```

In RHEL systems (Fedora, CentOS, etc.):

```
$ sudo dnf update
$ sudo dnf zlib-devel
```

In Arch Linux systems:

```
$ pacman -Syu
$ pacman -S zlib-devel
```

OpenSSL development library

In order to generate SHA-1 cryptographic hash values, Git uses the **OpenSSL development library**. Here are the commands for installing this library in some systems. This library is likely already installed in macOS and no action needs to be taken.

In Debian systems (Ubuntu, Mint, etc.):

```
$ sudo apt-get update
$ sudo apt-get install libssl-dev
```

In RHEL systems (Fedora, CentOS, etc.):

```
$ sudo dnf update
$ sudo dnf openssl-devel
```

In Arch Linux systems:

```
$ pacman -Syu
$ pacman -S openssl-devel
```

3.2 Installation steps

After checking that the required tools and libraries above are available in your system, or installing them if they are not, you are ready to install the original Git program. Here are the steps for installing the program.

Download the Git's original code package

Download the tar file babygit.tar.gz from the following link and save it in a directory of your choice:

https://initialcommit.com/baby-git-tar

Extract the files from the tar file

Go to the directory where you saved the tar file and extract its contents:

```
$ tar -xvzf babygit.tar.gz
```

After extracting the files from the archive, you will now have a directory named **`baby-git`** that contains the following files:

```
cache.h
cat-file.c
commit-tree.c
examples/babygit
examples/changelog
examples/hello.txt
examples/myfile1.txt
examples/myfile2.txt
init-db.c
LICENSE.txt
Makefile
MANIFEST
read-cache.c
read-tree.c
README.md
README.torvalds
show-diff.c
```

```
update-cache.c
write-tree.c
```

The `MANIFEST` file also lists the files that should be included in the package.

The `*.c` files and the `cache.h` file comprise Git's original C code. The `Makefile` will be used to compile and link this code. The `examples` directory contains some example user files and a shell script that will be used for the tutorial in Chapter 4.

Compile the code

Browse into the `baby-git/` directory in a terminal and compile the code by running the GNU `make` command.

```
$ cd baby-git
$ make
```

In a FreeBSD environment, the GNU version will probably be called gmake instead of make. In that case, use the `gmake` command:

```
$ gmake
```

Install Git's original commands

After a successful compilation, the following Git commands should be available in your directory:

```
cat-file
commit-tree
init-db
```

```
read-tree
show-diff
update-cache
write-tree
```

The last step would be to install these commands in a directory that is in your command search path (or **PATH**), i.e. the set of directories that are searched for executable commands.

By default, the Makefile provided will install these commands in your **$(HOME)/bin** directory, where **$(HOME)** is the path to your home directory. This would be the recommended install directory for the Git commands, so make sure that the directory **$(HOME)/bin** is in your command search path. Here are the steps to create the bin directory and to add it to your command path:

To create the **bin** directory in your home directory, type the following commands:

```
$ cd
$ mkdir bin
```

To add this directory to your command path, you need to add the **$(HOME)/bin** path to the **PATH** environment variable. You can do this by typing the following commands in order to set the **PATH** environment variable in the **.profile** file in your home directory:

```
$ cd
$ echo 'PATH="$HOME/bin:$PATH"' >> .profile
```

And then execute the commands in the **.profile** file:

```
$ source .profile
```

To check that your **$(HOME)/bin** directory has been added to the **PATH** environment variable, type the following command:

```
$ echo $PATH
```

You should see the path to your **$(HOME)/bin** directory at the beginning of the string that is displayed.

Finally, you are ready to install the Git commands in **$(HOME)/bin**. Use the following command to do so:

```
$ make install
```

In FreeBSD, use the **gmake** command:

```
$ gmake install
```

You can check if the commands were successfully installed in the **$(HOME)/bin** directory by using the **which** command. For example, to check if the init-db command was installed, type the following command:

```
$ which init-db
```

This should return the path to the init-db command if it was successfully installed.

4 Git's Original Command Tutorial

This chapter is a tutorial on how to use Git's original set of commands. It is assumed that the reader has successfully installed Git's original commands in a local machine by following the installation guide given in Chapter 3. It is also highly recommended that the reader peruse Chapter 2 and familiarize oneself with the concepts and terminology presented therein before going through this tutorial. The terms and concepts discussed in that chapter will be used often in this chapter.

Experienced Git users will notice some similarities in the basic functionalities of modern Git and its initial commit. In particular, the following commands have similar – but not identical – functionalities:

```
Original Git          Modern Git
--------              ---
init-db       ---->   git init
update-cache  ---->   git add
write-tree    ---->   git write-tree
commit-tree   ---->   git commit-tree
read-tree     ---->   git read-tree
show-diff     ---->   git diff
cat-file      ---->   git cat-file
```

This tutorial consists of three sections. First, we will show how the original 7 Git commands are used and explain their functions. Second, we will introduce a few other Git features. Finally, we will present some exercises in the use of the commands.

We will be using a terminal window in Unix-like environments to run the original Git commands. For Windows users, it is highly recommended that an MSYS2 environment be used. This is the same environment that was recommended in Chapter 3 for installing Git's first version in Windows. Please refer to Chapter 3 and the Appendix for more information about MSYS2.

4.1 Using the original Git commands

In this section, we will walk through the original Git command synopsis that was first presented at the end of Chapter 2. We will show how each command is used and then provide an explanation of what the command does.

Go to the directory where you extracted the **babygit.tar.gz** file and then go to the **examples/** directory below that directory. We will set up a Git repository in that directory and use the sample files that are found there.

```
$ cd examples
```

For this first section of the tutorial, we will be using the files **hello.txt** and **changelog**. Use the **cat** command to display the contents of the files:

```
$ cat hello.txt
Hello world!

$ cat changelog
Initial commit.
```

Initialize the repository

```
$ init-db
```

```
defaulting to private storage area
```

The first step in using Git's original repository is to initialize the object database and the cache directory. The **init-db** command creates the directory **.dircache** in the current working directory, in this case the **examples/** directory. The Git program uses this directory to store the repository cache, which is a binary file called **.dircache/index**. By default, the object database is also created in a directory called **.dircache/objects**.

Add a file to the cache

```
$ update-cache hello.txt
```

The **update-cache** command is used to add a file to the repository cache. In this case, we added the file **hello.txt** to the repository cache. As discussed in Chapter 2, when a file is added to the repository, a blob object corresponding to that file is added to the object database and the cache is updated with the file's metadata and the blob object's SHA-1 hash value.

Multiple files can be added to the repository by using the syntax:

```
$ update-cache <file 1> [<file 2>...]
```

where file 1, file 2, etc. are the paths of the files to be added to the repository cache.

Write a tree object to the object database

```
$ write-tree
60471dd2f6a67990755795708b2a09a5b3da505c
```

The `write-tree` command writes the tree object represented in the cache (index file) to the object database. It outputs the hash value of the tree object that was written. At this point, the cache contains information about one file, `hello.txt`, and thus the tree object that is written to the object database will also contain information about this one file.

Commit a tree object to the repository

```
$ commit-tree 60471dd2f6a67990755795708b2a09a5b3da505c < changelog
Committing initial tree 60471dd2f6a67990755795708b2a09a5b3da505c
deae7e7a5111831cd90e4f10379d798e135f734a
```

The `commit-tree` command commits a tree object to the repository. What this means is that a commit object is saved in the repository, and this commit object contains information about an existing tree object, as well as information about the user who committed the tree object and the time and date of the commit.

In its simplest form, the `commit-tree` command takes as an argument the hash value of the tree object to be committed. This is the same hash value that was output by the `write-tree` command.

In addition, the command also expects an input file whose contents will be used as the user comment in the commit object. This file is supplied to the command through the < redirection operator. In example above, we supplied the `changelog` file. This file can be any text file that contains a user's descriptive text about the tree object that was committed.

In summary, the basic syntax of the `commit-tree` command is:

```
$ commit-tree <tree hash value> < <comment file>
```

The command outputs the hash value of the commit object that results from a successful execution of the command. In this example, the hash value of the commit object is:

```
deae7e7a5111831cd90e4f10379d798e135f734a
```

Note that since the details of your commit will be different from the details in this example - that is, your user credentials and the commit time and date will be different - then the hash value of your commit object will be different from the hash value in this example. In the next step, make sure you substitute the actual hash value of your commit object into the command.

Get the contents of a commit object

```
$ cat-file deae7e7a5111831cd90e4f10379d798e135f734a
temp_git_file_LarhKM: commit
```

The contents of a commit object can be obtained using the `cat-file` command. This command can also be used to obtain the contents of a blob object, as we will see later. For this command, make sure you substitute the actual hash value of the commit object that you obtained in the previous step.

The `cat-file` command takes as input the hash value of an object and writes the object data into a uniquely and randomly named temporary file. It then outputs the name of the temporary file and the object type. In the example above, the filename is "temp_git_file_LarhKM" and the object type is "commit". Note that since the program randomly generates the filename, the filename that you actually get will be different from that shown above.

Use the `cat` command to display the contents of the file, making sure you substitute the actual filename you got into the command below:

```
$ cat temp_git_file_LarhKM
tree 60471dd2f6a67990755795708b2a09a5b3da505c
author Crusoe,,, <rcrusoe@island> Fri Apr 27 13:41:01 2018
committer Crusoe,,, <rcrusoe@island> Fri Apr 27 13:41:01 2018

Initial commit.
```

It can be seen from this output that a commit object contains the type and hash value of the tree object that was committed, information about the user who committed the tree object, the time and date of the commit, and the comment that was contained in the changelog file.

Read a tree object

```
$ read-tree 60471dd2f6a67990755795708b2a09a5b3da505c
100664 hello.txt (694cdbbdce662aa1060d07cba1d4e0cfeb822bee)
```

The **read-tree** command is used to display the contents of a tree object. It takes as input the hash value of the tree object.

For each file represented in the tree object, the **read-tree** command outputs the file mode, the file path, and the corresponding blob object's hash value. In the example above, 100664 is the file mode. It is an octal number that reflects the file type and permissions. In this case, it indicates that the file **hello.txt** is a regular file and that the owner and the group have read and write permissions, and others have write permission.

Note that this is the first time we're seeing the hash value of the blob object corresponding to the **hello.txt** file.

Read the contents of a blob object

```
$ cat-file 694cdbbdce662aa1060d07cba1d4e0cfeb822bee
temp_git_file_kEtFzM: blob
```

Now that we know the hash value of the blob object that was saved in the object database, we can use the **cat-file** command again to obtain the contents of this blob object. This time, the output of the command indicates that the object type is blob.

Use the **cat** command to display the contents of the file, making sure to substitute the actual filename you got into the command below:

```
$ cat temp_git_file_kEtFzM
Hello world!
```

Show the differences between blob objects and working files

```
$ show-diff
hello.txt: ok
```

For each file that is represented in the cache, the **show-diff** command displays the differences between the blob object and the working file. Remember that when a file is added to the repository or updated via the **update-cache** command, a blob object corresponding to that file is added to the object database and the cache is updated with the file's metadata and the blob object's hash value. It is this blob object to which the user's working file is compared.

In this case, since we have not made any changes to the file `hello.txt`, its contents and that of the blob object match, and the file metadata stored in the cache also match the working file's metadata, so the command outputs the message "ok".

4.2 Other features

In this section, we will introduce a few other features of Git's original codebase.

Parent commit objects

When committing a tree object using the `commit-tree` command, the user has the option of specifying parent commit objects. By specifying parent commits, one can track the history of changes to the tree object that was committed, effectively forming a branch. Logically, the parent commit object would be the commit object that resulted from the previous `commit-tree` command.

The function of parent commit objects in Git's original version is still very rudimentary. The user can specify a parent commit object when committing a tree object and this information will be stored in the child commit object to serve as a record. This information can then be displayed using the `cat-file` command in the same way it was used in the example given earlier in this chapter.

Apart from this, the Git program does not use parent commit objects for any other functionality and the user has to display the history of changes manually. Git's original version does not have the commands that are currently available in modern-day Git (git log and git branch) to conveniently display the history of changes and work with multiple branches.

The syntax for specifying parent commit objects is:

```
$ commit-tree <tree hash> [(-p <parent commit hash>)...] < changelog
```

where `<parent commit hash>` is the hash value of the parent commit object that the user wants to specify. Note that one can specify up to 16 parent commit objects in this command.

As an example of using a parent commit object, we will modify the **hello.txt** file, write a new tree object to the database, and then commit the tree using our previous commit object as the parent commit object. So let's say we change the content of **hello.txt** to:

```
$ cat hello.txt
Hello world of hobbits!
```

Since this is no longer the initial commit in the repository, we will also change the comment in the **changelog** to a more appropriate one:

```
$ cat changelog
Say hi to the hobbits too.
```

Then we again go through the process of updating the cache, writing a tree, and committing the tree, but this time using our previous commit as the parent commit object:

```
$ update-cache hello.txt
$ write-tree
a6c0cde3100d08bd95e0aaad7c92990dd2cb70b4

$ commit-tree a6c0cde3100d08bd95e0aaad7c92990dd2cb70b4 \
      -p deae7e7a5111831cd90e4f10379d798e135f734a < changelog
4d8c568418f727b9d246fe53d7131f88096f70e3
```

Again, the hash value of your commit objects will be different from the ones shown above. When following along in this tutorial, make sure you use the actual hash values that you get for your commit objects. In the case of the examples above, here are the hash values of our commit objects so far:

```
A: Initial commit of hello.txt with "Hello world!"
   deae7e7a5111831cd90e4f10379d798e135f734a

B: Modify hello.txt to "Hello world of hobbits!"
   4d8c568418f727b9d246fe53d7131f88096f70e3
```

For convenience, we will be referring to these commit objects as commit A and commit B, respectively. Again, note that commit A is the parent of commit B.

It is left as an exercise for the user to display the contents of the resulting commit object (see Exercise 1 in section 4.3).

Branches

Parent commit objects can be used to create a branch in a repository, although again in a very rudimentary way. A branch can be thought of as changes that are separate from the changes in the main branch. A branch can be created by specifying a parent commit object for a particular commit.

For example, let's say we want to make a change to the file **hello.txt** that is different from the one we made above in commit B. Of course, we can modify **hello.txt** again and make commit B the parent of the new commit object. But we could instead make commit A the parent of the new commit object, in which case we will be creating a branch in the repository.

Here is the different set of modifications we want:

```
$ cat hello.txt
Hello magical world!
```

```
$ cat changelog
Say hi to a magical world.
```

Again, we go through the process of updating the cache, writing a tree, and committing the tree, and again using commit A as the parent commit object:

```
$ update-cache hello.txt
$ write-tree
89d948b2a15dbc3fa55f747b1a15c0215f409824

$ commit-tree 89d948b2a15dbc3fa55f747b1a15c0215f409824 \
      -p deae7e7a5111831cd90e4f10379d798e135f734a < changelog
8d2d6bd787d8a1a9dae3ea20cfe1747b4baeee55
```

Now we have a new commit object, commit C:

```
C: Modify hello.txt to "Hello magical world!"
   8d2d6bd787d8a1a9dae3ea20cfe1747b4baeee55
```

The parent of commit C is commit A, which is also the parent of commit B. We can think of commit B and commit C as the roots of branches in our repository.

Merges

Merges are the logical consequence of having branches. At some point, a user might want to merge the branches in a repository. As with branches, this is done in Git's first version in a very rudimentary manner, but it can nevertheless serve as a learning tool for understanding merges.

NOTE Modern Git has several algorithms for computing

> merges, including the fast-forward merge, 3-way merge, recursive merge, octopus merge, and the latest and greatest ORT (ostensibly recursive's twin) merge. But Git's initial commit left the creation of merged content totally up to the user, as a manual process of editing the code in the working directory files.

In Git's initial commit, a merge of two branches can be performed by specifying the two parent commit objects of a commit object. For example, let's say we want to merge the changes made in commit B and commit C. That is, we edit the file **hello.txt** to contain:

```
$ cat hello.txt
Hello magical world of hobbits!
```

We also modify **changelog** to reflect this change in our comment:

```
$ cat changelog
Say hi to a magical world of hobbits.
```

The steps for updating the cache, writing a new tree, and committing the tree are similar to the ones shown above, but this time we specify both commit B and commit C as parent commit objects of the new commit object.

```
$ update-cache hello.txt
$ write-tree
80413994c212769a4bf45302647ca196759ff7fc

$ commit-tree 80413994c212769a4bf45302647ca196759ff7fc \
      -p 4d8c568418f727b9d246fe53d7131f88096f70e3 \
      -p 8d2d6bd787d8a1a9dae3ea20cfe1747b4baeee55 < changelog
```

```
2ffc11b4379bb0790d1e3a17f2d6ec124e47f743
```

Let's summarize the commit objects that we have:

```
A: Initial commit of hello.txt with "Hello world!"
   deae7e7a5111831cd90e4f10379d798e135f734a

B: Modify hello.txt to "Hello world of hobbits!"
   4d8c568418f727b9d246fe53d7131f88096f70e3

C: Modify hello.txt to "Hello magical world!"
   8d2d6bd787d8a1a9dae3ea20cfe1747b4baeee55

D: Merge commit B and commit C.
   Modify hello.txt to "Hello magical world of hobbits!"
   2ffc11b4379bb0790d1e3a17f2d6ec124e47f743
```

By specifying parent commit objects in the **commit-tree** command, we made two branches and then merged them. To summarize, commit A is the parent of commit B and commit C. Commit B and commit C are the starting points of two branches in our repository. Then we merged those two branches by specifying commit B and commit C as parent commit objects of commit D.

Again, it is important to remember that the hash values of your commit objects will be different from those shown in the examples above.

Database directory path

We mentioned earlier in this chapter that, by default, the Git program stores the object database in a directory called **.dircache/objects** that is created when the **init-db** command is used. It is possible for the user to specify a custom directory that contains the object database by using a Git environment variable called `SHA1_FILE_DIRECTORY`.

To specify a custom directory, one must first create a directory and copy an existing object database to this directory. The object database can be empty, i.e. contain no objects.

For example, we can create a directory called hobbits under the `examples/` directory and then copy the object database from the `.dircache/objects` directory:

```
$ mkdir hobbits
$ cp -ar .dircache/objects/* hobbits/
```

Then the `SHA1_FILE_DIRECTORY` environment variable can be set to the hobbits directory:

```
$ export SHA1_FILE_DIRECTORY=./hobbits
```

When the environment variable `SHA1_FILE_DIRECTORY` is set to a directory that contains a valid object database, all Git's original commands will use this object database instead of that contained in the default directory. Changing the value of `SHA1_FILE_DIRECTORY` is a useful way of having different object databases for the same working directory if needed.

Commit environment variables

Git's initial commit also has environment variables that a user can use to store information used in a commit object. These variables are:

```
COMMITTER_NAME to store the committer's name
COMMITTER_EMAIL to store the committer's email address
```

```
COMMITTER_DATE to store the commit date and time
```

The way to set the value of each variable is the same as that used above for the object database environment variable. For example, to set the user name to Bilbo Baggins, do the following:

```
$ export COMMITTER_NAME="Bilbo Baggins"
```

4.3 Exercises

In this section, we present some exercises to help the reader further familiarize themself with the original Git commands. Hopefully, this will encourage the user to explore the Git commands independently.

1. In the section about parent commit objects (section 4.2) we created commit B. Using this commit object's hash value, display the contents of this child commit object. Make sure that you use the hash value that you actually get in your own exercise and not the one given in the tutorial. What information about the parent commit object is stored in the child commit object? What is the comment stored in this child commit object?

2. Starting from the hash values you obtained for commit B and commit C, display the contents of the blob objects contained in their respective tree objects.

3. Using the hash value you obtained for commit D, display the contents of this commit object. How many parent commit objects are stored in commit D?

4. Starting from the hash value you obtained for commit D, display the contents of the blob object contained in its tree object. Compare this to the blob contents you obtained in Exercise 2.

5. The **touch** command updates the access and modification times of a file to the current time. Use the **touch** command to update the time stamp of the file **hello.txt**:

```
$ touch hello.txt
```

Then use the **show-diff** command to display the differences between the blob object and the working file. Note the output of the command. Why doesn't the output show "ok"?

6. Use your favorite text editor to edit the file **hello.txt** and change its contents. It's up to you as to what changes to make to the contents. Use the **show-diff** command to display the differences between the blob object and the working file. Now update the cache to reflect the changes you made to **hello.txt**. Then Use the **show-diff** command again to display the differences between the blob object and the working file.

7. In the **examples/** directory, there is a shell script named **babygit**. This script automates a Git workflow. Browse the script and try to understand it. It makes use of the two user files **myfile1.txt** and **myfile2.txt**. These texts are from the first chapter of Robinson Crusoe. They might contain a couple of typos. Once you have browsed the script, try running it and see if you understand what it is doing. To run the script, type:

```
$ ./babygit
```

Part 2: Git's Original C Code

In the second part of this guidebook, we will be studying the original Git C code itself to help the reader understand how a program like Git is actually coded under the hood. For each of the 7 original Git commands, we will look at the algorithms of the more salient functions and look at some code snippets. All code snippets are extracts from Git's initial commit source code, which can be found at the following link:

https://bitbucket.org/jacobstopak/baby-git/src/master/

Each of the 7 original Git commands has a specific source code file independent from the other commands. Functions and external variables that are used in common by the commands are declared and defined in the header file `cache.h` and in the source file `read-cache.c`. These files will be discussed prior to the 7 commands.

The line numbers that are included in the code snippets found in the following chapters are the actual line numbers in the source files that accompany this guidebook. By using the actual line numbers in the code snippets, the reader can easily navigate to the lines of code in the source files that are referenced in the text of the chapters.

Git's initial commit source code that accompanies this guidebook is the same code that comprised the initial commit of the Git code in terms of the logic, structure, and implementation. For the purposes of this guidebook, the code has, however, been liberally annotated. The formatting was also made more consistent to make the code easier to read. A couple of bug fixes were also made. Finally, some lines of code were added so that the program would compile and run under a desktop Windows environment. None of these changes affected the essential functioning and design of the original code in any way.

5 cache.h

Git's initial commit has a **C header file** named **`cache.h`** that is included in all the source files via the **`#include`** preprocessing directive. This file contains other include directives of library header files, macro definitions, declarations of external variables and structure templates, and function prototypes.

NOTE When a C header file is included in another file, the C preprocessor essentially copies and pastes the header file code at the location it is included in the other file. This makes header files a useful place to store reusable code bits to be included in many or all other source files.

5.1 Object database path macros

There are two macros defined in the header that are used by the program to determine where the object database is stored. These macros are:

```
/*
 * If desired, you can use an environment variable to set a custom path to the
 * object store.
 */
#define DB_ENVIRONMENT "SHA1_FILE_DIRECTORY"

/*
 * The default path to the object store.
 */
#define DEFAULT_DB_ENVIRONMENT ".dircache/objects"
```

NOTE A **macro** in C is just a named bit of code. At compilation time, the C preprocessor will parse out any instances of the specified name in the source files, and replace them with the corresponding bit of code defined by the macro.

By default, the object database is stored in the path defined by the **DEFAULT_DB_ENVIRONMENT** macro, which is **.dircache/objects**. The **DB_ENVIRONMENT** macro is defined as **SHA1_FILE_DIRECTORY**, which is an environment variable that the user can use to specify a custom object database.

5.2 Cache structures

The templates of the **cache_header** and **cache_entry** structures are declared in the **cache.h** header file. These structures are used to store the repository cache.

The cache_header structure template is:

```
/* Template of the header structure that identifies a set of cache entries. */
struct cache_header {
    /* Constant across all headers, to validate authenticity. */
    unsigned int signature;
    /* Stores the version of Git that created the cache. */
    unsigned int version;
    /* The number of cache entries in the cache. */
    unsigned int entries;
    /* The SHA1 hash that identifies the cache. */
    unsigned char sha1[20];
};
```

One can see that the cache header structure comprises a signature, a version, the number of cache entries, and the SHA-1 hash that identifies the cache file. The signature is a constant whose value is also given in the header file via the **CACHE_SIGNATURE** macro:

```
/* This `CACHE_SIGNATURE` is hardcoded to be loaded into all cache headers. */
#define CACHE_SIGNATURE 0x44495243   /* Linus Torvalds: "DIRC" */
```

The **cache_entry** structure template is:

```
118 /*
119  * Template of the cache entry structure that stores information about the
120  * corresponding user file in the working directory.
121  */
122 struct cache_entry {
123     struct cache_time ctime;    /* Time of file's last status change. */
124     struct cache_time mtime;    /* Time of file's last modification. */
125     unsigned int st_dev;        /* Device ID of device containing the file. */
126 
127     /*
128      * The file serial number, which distinguishes this file from all
129      * other files on the same device.
130      */
131     unsigned int st_ino;
132 
133     /*
134      * Specifies the mode of the file. This includes information about the
135      * file type and permissions.
136      */
137     unsigned int st_mode;
138     unsigned int st_uid;       /* The user ID of the file's owner. */
139     unsigned int st_gid;       /* The group ID of the file. */
140     unsigned int st_size;      /* The size of a regular file in bytes. */
141     unsigned char sha1[20];    /* The SHA1 hash of deflated blob object. */
142     unsigned short namelen;    /* The filename or path length. */
143     unsigned char name[0];     /* The filename or path. */
144 };
```

One can see that the **cache_entry** structure is used to store information or metadata about the file that corresponds to the cache entry. Note line 141, which is the structure member that stores the 20-byte representation of the SHA-1 hash of the deflated blob object that corresponds to the cache entry. This hash is used to index the blob object in the object database.

The **cache_time** structure used in the **cache_entry** template is also declared in the header file. Its members represent a time stamp's second and nanosecond portions:

```
/*
 * Template of a time structure for storing the time stamps of actions taken on
 * a file corresponding to a cache entry. For example, the time the file was
 * modified. For some info on file times, see:
```

```
 * https://www.quora.com/What-is-the-difference-between-mtime-atime-and-ctime
 */
struct cache_time {
    unsigned int sec;
    unsigned int nsec;
};
```

5.3 External variables

Git's initial commit uses external variables that are defined in the `read-cache.c` source file and declared in the header file for inclusion in the other source files. These external variables are:

```
/* The path to the object store. */
const char *sha1_file_directory;
/* An array of pointers to cache entries. */
struct cache_entry **active_cache;
/* The number of entries in the `active_cache` array. */
unsigned int active_nr;
/* The maximum number of elements the active_cache array can hold. */
unsigned int active_alloc;
```

5.4 Function prototypes

The following are function prototypes in the header file. These functions are used by the different Git commands and are defined in the source file `read-cache.c`.

```
/*
 * Read the contents of the `.dircache/index` file into the `active_cache`
 * array.
 */
extern int read_cache(void);

/*
 * Linus Torvalds: Return a statically allocated filename matching the SHA1
 * signature
 */
extern char *sha1_file_name(unsigned char *sha1);

```

```
/* Linus Torvalds: Write a memory buffer out to the SHA1 file. */
extern int write_sha1_buffer(unsigned char *sha1, void *buf,
                             unsigned int size);

/*
 * Linus Torvalds: Read and unpack a SHA1 file into memory, write memory to a
 * SHA1 file.
 */
extern void *read_sha1_file(unsigned char *sha1, char *type,
                            unsigned long *size);
extern int write_sha1_file(char *buf, unsigned len);

/* Linus Torvalds: Convert to/from hex/sha1 representation. */
extern int get_sha1_hex(char *hex, unsigned char *sha1);
/* Linus Torvalds: static buffer! */
extern char *sha1_to_hex(unsigned char *sha1);

/* Print usage message to standard error stream. */
extern void usage(const char *err);
```

6 read-cache.c

The `read-cache.c` source file defines various functions that are used program-wide in Git's original codebase. It also contains definitions of external (or global) variables used by the program. Please refer to Chapter 5, `cache.h`, for a list of these functions and variables. We will discuss the more important of these functions here in preparation for the discussion in the next chapters.

6.1 read_cache

Synopsis

```
int entries;
entries = read_cache();
```

Description

The `read_cache` function reads the cache entries in the `.dircache/index` cache file into the `active_cache` array.

Function prototype

```
extern int read_cache(void);
```

Algorithm

The `read_cache` function first gets the path to the object database. It then opens the `.dircache/index` cache file for reading. It uses the the `fstat()` function to get information about the cache file and to store it in a `stat` structure.

NOTE `fstat()` is a C function that is used to retrieve information about a file that is already referenced by an existing **file descriptor**. A file descriptor is just an integer that the OS has mapped to a previously opened file, often using the `open()` function in C. `fstat()` will retrieve that file's metadata, including file size, type, permissions, and more. This information is stored in a C `stat()` structure for later user.

If the size of the cache file is valid, then the contents of the cache file is mapped to memory using the `mmap` function for program access. The cache header is then validated using the `verify_hdr` function. If the header is not valid, the memory that was mapped to the cache file is unmapped, an error message is displayed, and the program returns a -1.

If the cache header is valid, the number of cache entries in the cache is then stored in the `active_nr` global variable and the cache entries are stored in the `active_cache` array, the pointer to which is also a global variable. Finally, `active_nr` is returned to the calling program.

Return value

On success, `read_cache` returns the number of cache entries in the cache file. On failure, it returns -1.

Code snippets

The `mmap` function is often used in Git's initial commit to map file contents to memory. Here is the line in the `read_cache` function that does this:

```
map = mmap(NULL, size, PROT_READ, MAP_PRIVATE, fd, 0);
```

Here, **fd** is the file descriptor for the cache file and **size** is the size of the cache file, which will be the amount of data to map to memory. The **mmap** function returns a pointer to the start of the memory location and this is stored in the **map** pointer. This memory is just the buffered bytestream of the binary file content that was read. The **PROT_READ** flag indicates that the memory can be read, and the **MAP_PRIVATE** flag indicates that changes to the mapped data should not be written back to the file.

The following is the portion of the code that stores the number of cache entries in the **active_nr** global variable and the cache entries in the **active_cache** array.

```
/* The number of cache entries in the cache. */
active_nr = hdr->entries;
/* The maximum number of elements the active_cache array can hold. */
active_alloc = alloc_nr(active_nr);

/*
 * Allocate memory for the `active_cache` array. Memory is allocated for
 * an array of `active_alloc` number of elements, each one having the size
 * of a `cache_entry` structure.
 */
active_cache = calloc(active_alloc, sizeof(struct cache_entry *));

/*
 * `offset` is an index to the next byte of `map` to read. In this case,
 * set it to the beginning of the first cache entry after the header.
 */
offset = sizeof(*hdr);

/*
 * Add each cache entry into the `active_cache` array and increase the
 * `offset` index by the size of the current cache entry.
 */
for (i = 0; i < hdr->entries; i++) {
    struct cache_entry *ce = map + offset;
    offset = offset + ce_size(ce);
    active_cache[i] = ce;
```

```
}

/* Return the number of cache entries in the cache. */
return active_nr;
```

Since **active_nr** and **active_cache** are global variables, these are available to other functions for further processing.

See Chapter 5, **cache.h**, for an explanation of the structure of Git's original cache.

6.2 write_sha1_file

Synopsis

```
char *buf;
unsigned int len;
...
write_sha1_file(buf, len);
```

Description

The **write_sha1_file** function deflates an object, calculates the hash value, and then calls the **write_sha1_buffer** function to write the deflated object to the object database.

Function prototype

```
extern int write_sha1_file(char *buf, unsigned len);
```

Algorithm

The **write_sha1_file** function first deflates an object that is stored in the **buf** buffer using zlib library functions. The SHA-1 hash value of the deflated object is then calculated using OpenSSL library functions. Finally, the compressed object is written to the object database using the hexadecimal representation of its SHA-1 hash as index, and this hash is displayed on screen.

Return value

On success, `write_sha1_file` returns 0. On failure, it returns -1.

Code snippets

All objects in Git are deflated before writing them to the object database. Here is the portion of the code in the `write_sha1_file` function that calls zlib functions to deflate an object:

```
/* Initialize the zlib stream to contain null characters. */
memset(&stream, 0, sizeof(stream));

/*
 * Initialize compression stream for optimized compression
 * (as opposed to speed).
 */
deflateInit(&stream, Z_BEST_COMPRESSION);
/* Determine upper bound on compressed size. */
size = deflateBound(&stream, len);
/* Allocate `size` bytes of space to store the next compressed output. */
compressed = malloc(size);

/* Specify buf as location of the next input to the compression stream. */
stream.next_in = buf;
/* Number of bytes available as input for next compression. */
stream.avail_in = len;
/* Specify compressed as location to write the next compressed output. */
stream.next_out = compressed;
/* Number of bytes available for storing the next compressed output. */
stream.avail_out = size;

/* Compress the content of buf, i.e., compress the object. */
while (deflate(&stream, Z_FINISH) == Z_OK)
/* Linus Torvalds: nothing */;

/*
 * Free memory structures that were dynamically allocated for the
```

```
601  * compression.
602  */
603 deflateEnd(&stream);
604 /* Get size of total compressed output. */
605 size = stream.total_out;
```

The function first initializes stream, which is a zlib **z_stream** structure (lines 574 and 580). It then allocates memory for storing the compressed output (line 584). The members of the stream structure are then set (lines 586 to 593): The memory location of the next input to compress, the number of bytes available as input for the next compression, the location to write the next compressed output, and the number of bytes available for storing the next compressed output. The input stream is then deflated (lines 595 to 597). Finally, the memory structures that were used for the compression are freed (line 603) and the total size of the compressed output is stored in the **size** variable (line 605).

After an object is deflated, its SHA-1 hash value is always calculated. The 40-character hexadecimal representation of this hash value is used to index and reference the object in the object store. Here is the portion of code in **write_sha1_file** that calculates the SHA-1 hash value of an object:

```
607 /* Initialize the SHA context structure. */
608 SHA1_Init(&c);
609 /* Calculate hash of the compressed output. */
610 SHA1_Update(&c, compressed, size);
611 /* Store the SHA1 hash of the compressed output in `sha1`.  */
612 SHA1_Final(sha1, &c);
```

The SHA context structure **c** is first initialized (line 608). The SHA-1 hash of the compressed output is then calculated (line 610). The final 20-byte hash value of the deflated object is then stored in the 20-byte array **sha1.** Then the **c** SHA context structure is erased (line 612).

Finally, the **write_sha1_buffer** function is called to write the object to the object database, and then the 40-character hexadecimal representation of the object's SHA-1 hash is displayed on screen:

```
614 /* Write the compressed object to the object store. */
615 if (write_sha1_buffer(sha1, compressed, size) < 0)
616     return -1;
617 /*
618  * Display the 40-character hexadecimal representation of the object's
619  * SHA1 hash value.
620  */
621 printf("%s\n", sha1_to_hex(sha1));
```

In line 621, the **sha1_to_hex** function is used to convert the 20-byte representation of the hash value to a 40-character hexadecimal representation.

6.3 read_sha1_file

Synopsis

```
char sha1_hex[] = "694cdbbdce662aa1060d07cba1d4e0cfeb822bee";
unsigned char sha1[20];
char type[20];
unsigned long size;
void *buf;
get_sha1_hex(sha1_hex, sha1);
buf = read_sha1_file(sha1, type, &size);
```

Description

The **read_sha1_file** function locates an object in the object database using the 40-character hexadecimal representation of its SHA-1 hash, reads and inflates the object, then returns the inflated object data without the prepended metadata.

Function prototype

```
extern void *read_sha1_file(unsigned char *sha1, char *type,
                            unsigned long *size);
```

Algorithm

The `read_sha1_file` function does the reverse steps of the `write_sha1_file` function. It first calls the `sha1_file_name` function to build the path of an object in the object database using the object's SHA-1 hash. The object is then opened for reading and its metadata is obtained using the `fstat` function and is stored in the `st` stat structure.

The object contents are then mapped into memory using the `mmap` function. These contents are then inflated using zlib library functions and the inflated contents are initially stored in a buffer that has a size of 8192 bytes.

After inflation, the object type and object data size are read from the buffer and stored in the corresponding variables that were passed as parameters. Next, using the `memcpy` function, the part of the buffer that contains only the deflated data is copied to another buffer that has a size equal to the object data size.

If the size of the inflated output is less than the size of the object data, the remaining uninflated object data is inflated. Finally, the pointer to the buffer containing the entire inflated object data is returned to the calling program.

Return value

On success, `read_sha1_file` returns a pointer to the memory location that contains the inflated object data. On failure, it returns `NULL`.

Code snippets

All objects are inflated after being opened. Here is the part of the **read_sha1_file** function that inflates an object:

```
502 /* Initialize the zlib stream to contain null characters. */
503 memset(&stream, 0, sizeof(stream));
504 /* Set map as location of the next input to the inflation stream. */
505 stream.next_in = map;
506 /* Number of bytes available as input for next inflation. */
507 stream.avail_in = st.st_size;
508 /* Set `buffer` as the location to write the next inflated output. */
509 stream.next_out = buffer;
510 /* Number of bytes available for storing the next inflated output. */
511 stream.avail_out = sizeof(buffer);
512
513 /* Initialize the stream for decompression. */
514 inflateInit(&stream);
515 /* Decompress the object contents and store return code in `ret`. */
516 ret = inflate(&stream, 0);
```

The function first initializes the zlib **z_stream** structure stream to contain null characters (line 503). The members of the stream structure are then set (lines 504 to 511): The memory location of the next input to inflate, the number of bytes available as input for the next inflation, the location to write the next inflated output, and the number of bytes available for storing the next inflated output. The zlib **z_stream** structure is then initialized for inflation (line 514), and then the input stream is inflated (line 516).

Later on, the code checks if all the object data was inflated, because if the size of **buffer** was less than the size of the inflated object data, then the inflate command in line 516 stops even if there is still data left to be inflated. Here is the part of the code that copies the inflated data to a new buffer, **buf**, that has a size equal to the expected size of inflated object data (line 541), and then checks if there is still data left to be inflated (line 545):

```
537 /*
538  * Copy the inflated object data from buffer to buf, i.e, without the
539  * prepended metadata (the object type and expected object data size).
540  */
541 memcpy(buf, buffer + bytes, stream.total_out - bytes);
542 /* The size of the inflated data without the prepended metadata. */
543 bytes = stream.total_out - bytes;
544 /* Continue inflation if not all data has been inflated. */
545 if (bytes < *size && ret == Z_OK) {
546     stream.next_out = buf + bytes;
547     stream.avail_out = *size - bytes;
548     while (inflate(&stream, Z_FINISH) == Z_OK)
549         /* Linus Torvalds: nothing */;
550 }
551 /* Free memory structures that were used for the inflation. */
552 inflateEnd(&stream);
```

In line 545, `size` is the expected size of the inflated object data. This was read from the stored object metadata.

Lines 546 to 548 inflate any remaining uninflated object data. Finally, the memory structures that were used for the inflation are freed (line 552).

6.4 write_sha1_buffer

Synopsis

```
unsigned char sha1[20];
void *buf;
unsigned int size;
...
write_sha1_buffer(sha1, buf, size);
```

Description

The `write_sha1_buffer` function writes a deflated object to the object database, using the object's SHA-1 hash value as index.

Function prototype

```
extern int write_sha1_buffer(unsigned char *sha1, void *buf,
                             unsigned int size);
```

Algorithm

The `write_sha1_buffer` function first calls the `sha1_file_name` function to build the path of the object in the object database using the object's SHA-1 hash. A new file with this path is then opened for writing in the object database. Finally, the deflated object is written to this path using the `write` function.

Return value

On success, `write_sha1_buffer` returns 0. On failure, it returns -1.

Code snippets

The line of code that writes the deflated object to the object store is in line 652:

```
652 write(fd, buf, size);    /* Write the object to the object store. */
```

Here, `fd` is the file descriptor of the object, `buf` is the buffer that contains the deflated object, and `size` is the size of the deflated object.

6.5 sha1_to_hex

Synopsis

```
unsigned char sha1[20];
...
printf("SHA-1 hash: %s\n", sha1_to_hex(sha1));
```

Description

The **sha1_to_hex** function converts a 20-byte representation of an SHA-1 hash value to the equivalent 40-character hexadecimal representation.

Function prototype

```
char *sha1_to_hex(unsigned char *sha1);
```

Algorithm

The **sha1_to_hex** function first defines a lookup character array called **hex** for getting the hexadecimal representation of a number from 0 to 15. It then loops through the 20 numbers (ranging from 0 to 255) in the 20-character **sha1** unsigned character array and converts each one to its two-digit hexadecimal representation (ranging from 00 to ff).

Return value

The **sha1_to_hex** function returns a pointer to the character array containing the hexadecimal representation of a given SHA-1 hash.

Code snippets

Here is the short **sha1_to_hex** function:

```
332 char *sha1_to_hex(unsigned char *sha1)
333 {
334     /* String for storing the 40-character hexadecimal representation. */
335     static char buffer[50];
336     /*
337      * Lookup array for getting the hexadecimal representation of a number
338      * from 0 to 15.
339      */
340     static const char hex[] = "0123456789abcdef";
341     /* Pointer used for filling up the buffer string. */
342     char *buf = buffer;
343     int i;
344 
345     /*
346      * Get the two-digit hexadecimal representation (ranging from 00 to ff) of
347      * a number (ranging from 0 to 255).
348      */
349     for (i = 0; i < 20; i++) {
350         unsigned int val = *sha1++;    /* Get the current number. */
351         *buf++ = hex[val >> 4];        /* Convert the 4 high bits to hex. */
352         *buf++ = hex[val & 0xf];       /* Convert the 4 low bits to hex. */
353     }
354     return buffer;   /* Return the hexadecimal representation. */
355 }
```

Line 335 defines the character array where the 40-character hexadecimal representation of a given SHA-1 hash will be stored, and line 340 defines the **hex** lookup character array. The character pointer **buf** defined in line 342 serves as an index for filling up the buffer array. It is initially set to the first character of **buffer**.

The conversion from the 20-byte representation of the SHA-1 hash value to the equivalent 40-character hexadecimal representation is done in lines 349 to 353. In this loop, each number in the **sha1** array, which can range from 0 to 255, is converted to a two-digit hexadecimal number ranging from 00 to ff.

Lines 351 and 352 perform bitwise operations on the current number, **val**. In line 351, **val** is right shifted by 4 bits and then this is used as an index to the **hex** array. This means that the 4 high bits of **val** are the first to be converted to a hexadecimal number and then stored in the **buffer** array.

The `buf` index is then incremented and then the bitwise and of `val` with 0xf is used as an index to the `hex` array. This means that the 4 low bits of `val` are converted to a hexadecimal number and then stored into `buffer`.

6.6 get_sha1_hex

Synopsis

```
char sha1_hex[] = "694cdbbdce662aa1060d07cba1d4e0cfeb822bee";
unsigned char sha1[20];
get_sha1_hex(sha1_hex, sha1);
```

Description

The `get_sha1_hex` function converts a 40-character hexadecimal representation of an SHA-1 hash value to the equivalent 20-byte representation.

Function prototype

```
extern int get_sha1_hex(char *sha1_hex, unsigned char *sha1);
```

Algorithm

The `get_sha1_hex` function loops through the 20 two-digit hexadecimal numbers (ranging from 00 to ff) in the given 40-character representation of a SHA-1 hash value and converts this number to the equivalent decimal number (ranging from 0 to 255). The decimal equivalents are stored in the `sha1` unsigned char array.

Return value

On success, the **get_sha1_hex** function returns 0. On failure, it returns -1.

Code snippets

Here is the entirety of the short **get_sha1_hex** function:

```
302 int get_sha1_hex(char *hex, unsigned char *sha1)
303 {
304     int i;
305     /*
306      * Convert each two-digit hexadecimal number (ranging from 00 to ff) to a
307      * decimal number (ranging from 0 to 255).
308      */
309     for (i = 0; i < 20; i++) {
310         /*
311          * The decimal equivalent of the first hexadecimal digit will form
312          * the 4 high bits of val; that of the second hex digit will form the
313          * 4 low bits.
314          */
315         unsigned int val = (hexval(hex[0]) << 4) | hexval(hex[1]);
316         /* Return -1 if val is larger than 255. */
317         if (val & ~0xff)
318             return -1;
319         *sha1++ = val;     /* Store val in sha1 array. */
320         hex += 2;          /* Get next two-digit hexadecimal number. */
321     }
322     return 0;
323 }
```

In line 315, **hexval** is a function in **read-cache.c** that converts a hexadecimal symbol (0 to 9, a to f, or A to F), to its decimal equivalent (0 to 15).

In this same line, bitwise operations are again performed. The first digit, **hex[0]**, in the current two-digit hexadecimal number is left shifted by 4 bits and converted to a decimal number. Then the second digit, **hex[1]** is converted to a decimal number. The bitwise or of the two numbers is then taken to complete the decimal number corresponding to the current two-digit hexadecimal number. This means that the decimal equivalent of the first hexadecimal digit will form the 4 high bits of `val`, and that of the second hexadecimal digit will form the 4 low bits.

6.7 sha1_file_name

Synopsis

```
unsigned char sha1[20];
....
char *filename = sha1_file_name(sha1);
```

Description

The `sha1_file_name` function builds the path of an object in the object database using the object's SHA-1 hash value.

Function prototype

```
extern char *sha1_file_name(unsigned char *sha1);
```

Algorithm

The `sha1_file_name` first gets the path to the object database and copies it into a character array called **base.** A / is then written in the first and fourth elements of the base array after the object database path, leaving two uninitialized array elements in between the two / characters.

These two array elements are then filled with the first two characters of the 40-character representation of the given SHA-1 hash value in the `sha1` array. The remaining 38 characters of the hexadecimal representation are then written to the base array to form the filename of the object and to complete the path to the object in the object database. Finally, **base** is returned to the calling program.

Return value

The **sha1_file_name** function returns a pointer to a string containing the constructed path of an object in the object database.

Code snippets

Here is the part of the code that fills in the base character array with the directory and filename of the object using the object's SHA-1 hash value.

```
/*
 * Fill in the rest of the object path (object directory and filename)
 * using the object's SHA1 hash value.
 *
 * Convert each number in the sha1 array (ranging from 0 to 255) to a
 * two-digit hexadecimal number (ranging from 00 to ff). The first
 * two-digit hexadecimal number will form part of the object directory.
 * The rest of the two-digit hexadecimal numbers will comprise the object
 * filename.
 */
for (i = 0; i < 20; i++) {
    /*
     * Lookup array for getting the hexadecimal representation of a
     * number from 0 to 15.
     */
    static char hex[] = "0123456789abcdef";
    /* Get the current number from sha1. */
    unsigned int val = sha1[i];
    /*
     * Set the index of the base array. This will be name + 0, name + 3,
     * name + 5, name + 7,..., name + 39.
     */
    char *pos = name + i*2 + (i > 0);
    *pos++ = hex[val >> 4];    /* Convert the 4 high bits to hex. */
    *pos = hex[val & 0xf];     /* Convert the 4 low bits to hex. */
```

```
428 }
```

The `pos` character pointer in line 425 serves as an index to the base array in which the path of the object is being constructed. The right-hand side of the equation in this line consists of three terms. The `name` variable is a pointer to the byte in `base` where the two-character object directory starts. The second term, `i*2` takes on the values 0, 2, 4, 6, ..., 38.

The third term, `(i > 0)` has a value of 1 when `i` is greater than 0, and 0 otherwise. Thus, the `pos` index takes on the values `name`, `name + 3`, `name + 5`, `name + 7`, ..., `name + 39`. The `name + 2` index is skipped because a `/` character was already written there to separate the object directory from the object filename.

Lines 426 and 427 are similar to what was done in the `sha1_to_hex` function, where the 4 high bits of of `val` are the first to be converted to a hexadecimal number and then stored in the base array, followed by the 4 low bits.

7 init-db.c

7.1 main

Synopsis

```
init-db
```

Description

The `init-db` command creates a hidden directory where the repository cache will be stored. If needed, it also creates an object database in this directory.

Algorithm

The code first creates the `.dircache` hidden directory under the current working directory. It prints an error message and exits if the directory already exists.

It then checks if the environment variable `SHA1_FILE_DIRECTORY` is defined. This environment variable can be used to specify the path of an existing valid object database. If the environment variable is defined and is set to an existing directory, then the code terminates successfully. If not, then it creates the directory `.dircache/objects`, where the object database will be stored.

Under the `.dircache/objects` directory, the code then creates 256 directories named from 00 to ff, corresponding to the 256 values that a two-digit hexadecimal number can represent.

Return value

On success, **init-db** returns 0. On failure, it returns 1.

Code snippets

The **init-db.c** source code is a short file that consists of a main function only. Here is the part of the code that creates the 256 directories of the object database under the default **.dircache/objects** directory:

```
225 /*
226  * Execute this loop 256 times to create the 256 subdirectories inside the
227  * `.dircache/objects/` directory. The subdirectories will be named `00`
228  * to `ff`, which are the hexadecimal representations of the numbers 0 to
229  * 255. Each subdirectory will be used to hold the objects whose SHA1 hash
230  * values in hexadecimal representation start with those two digits.
231  */
232 for (i = 0; i < 256; i++) {
233     /*
234      * Convert `i` to a two-digit hexadecimal number and append it to the
235      * path variable after the `.dircache/objects/` part. That way, each
236      * time through the loop we build up one of the following paths:
237      * `.dircache/objects/00`, `.dircache/objects/01`, ...,
238      * `.dircache/objects/fe`, `.dircache/objects/ff`.
239      */
240     sprintf(path+len, "/%02x", i);
241 
242     /*
243      * Attempt to create the current subdirectory. If it fails, `mkdir()`
244      * will return -1 and the program will print a message and exit.
245      */
246     if (MKDIR(path) < 0) {
247         if (errno != EEXIST) {
248             perror(path);
249             exit(1);
250         }
251     }
252 }
```

In line 240, path is a character array for storing the path to the directory that will be created. Before entering the for loop, it is set to the default object database path, `.dircache/objects`. The variable `len` is the length of this default path. The `sprintf` function in line 240 thus writes a forward slash `/` and the hexadecimal representation of the number `i` to path after the `.dircache/objects` string.

The directory is created in line 246, where `MKDIR` is a system-dependent macro defined at the beginning of the source code. For Unix-like systems, this macro is defined as the `mkdir` command:

```
38 #define MKDIR( path ) ( mkdir( path, 0700 ) )
```

The `mkdir` command in line 38 creates the path directory with its permission bits set to `0700`, i.e. only the owner has read, write, and execute permissions.

8 update-cache.c

In this chapter, we will discuss some of the more salient functions in the `update-cache.c` source file.

8.1 main

Synopsis

```
update-cache <path>...
```

Description

The `update_cache` command updates the repository cache and the object database with the files specified by the user as command line arguments. For each of these files, a blob object associated with that file is created and added to the object database, and the file metadata is added to the cache stored in the binary file `.dircache/index`.

Algorithm

The main function first calls the **`read_cache`** function to read the cache entries in the **`.dircache/index`** cache file into the **`active_cache`** array (see Chapter 6 for details of the **`read_cache`** function). A new cache lock file called **`.dircache/index.lock`** is then created and opened.

For each input file represented in the cache, the code checks if the file's path is valid using the **`verify_path`** function. Paths that are absolute paths, paths that contain dots (hidden files or paths that are above the working directory), double slashes, or a trailing slash are not allowed.

For each file with a valid path, the **add_file_to_cache** function is called. This function stores the file metadata in a **cache_entry** structure, and makes function calls to write the corresponding blob object to the object database and to insert the cache entry into the **active_cache** array lexicographically.

After all the valid files have been processed (blob object added to object database and cache entry added to the **active_cache** array), the cache header and the cache entries in the **active_cache** array are written to the **.dircache/index.lock** file using the **write_cache** function. Finally, the **.dircache/index.lock** file is moved to the **.dircache/index** cache file, replacing the existing cache file if any.

Return value

On success, the **main** function returns 0. On failure, it returns -1.

Code snippets

Here is the part of the **main** function that loops through the paths in the command line argument and updates the **active_cache** array with the corresponding cache entry and the object database with the corresponding blob object:

```
for (i = 1 ; i < argc; i++) {
    /* Store the ith path that was passed as a command line argument. */
    char *path = argv[i];

    /*
     * Verify the path. If the path is not valid, continue to the next
     * file.
     */
    if (!verify_path(path)) {
        fprintf(stderr, "Ignoring path %s\n", argv[i]);
        continue;
    }

    /*
     * This calls `add_file_to_cache()`, which does a few things:
     *     1) Opens the file at `path`.
```

```
718      *       2) Gets information about the file and stores the file
719      *          metadata in a cache_entry structure.
720      *       3) Calls the index_fd() function to construct a corresponding
721      *          blob object and write it to the object database.
722      *       4) Calls the add_cache_entry() function to insert the cache
723      *          entry into the active_cache array lexicographically.
724      *
725      * If any of these steps leads to a nonzero return code (i.e. fails),
726      * jump to the `out` label below.
727      */
728     if (add_file_to_cache(path)) {
729         fprintf(stderr, "Unable to add %s to database\n", path);
730         goto out;
731     }
732 }
```

Lines 702 and 704 contain the conventional arguments to the `main` function, `argc` and `argv`, that are respectively the number of command line arguments and an array of pointers to strings that contain the command line arguments. In this case, `argv[0]` points to the `update-cache` string, and the remaining strings are the file paths specified by the user.

8.2 add_file_to_cache

Synopsis

```
char *path = argv[1];
add_file_to_cache(path);
```

Description

The `add_file_to_cache` function stores a file's metadata in a `cache_entry` structure, then calls the `index_fd` function to construct a blob object and write it to the object store, and the `add_cache_entry` function to insert the cache entry into the `active_cache` array lexicographically.

Function prototype

```
static int add_file_to_cache(char *path);
```

Algorithm

The **add_file_to_cache** function first opens the file in the specified path for reading and checks if the file exists in the working directory. If it does not and there is a corresponding entry in the cache, then that entry is removed from the **active_cache** array using the **remove_file_from_cache** function.

If the file exists, then the file metadata is obtained using the **fstat** function and is stored in a **stat** structure. The following file metadata are then stored in a **cache_entry** structure:

```
time of last status change
time of last modification
device ID of device containing the file
file inode number
file mode (type and permissions)
file user ID
file group ID
file size in bytes
file path length
file path
```

The blob object corresponding to the file is then created and written to the object database using the **index_fd** function. This function also adds the deflated blob object's SHA-1 hash value to the **cache_entry** structure. The cache entry is then inserted into the **active_cache** array by calling the **add_cache_entry** function. The cache entry's position in the array is determined by the lexicographic rank of the file's path in the array.

Return value

On success, **add_file_to_cache** returns the return value of the **add_cache_entry** function. On failure, it returns -1.

Code snippets

Here is the part of the code that opens a user file for reading and stores the file metadata to a **cache_entry** structure:

```
/* File descriptor for the file to add to the cache. */
int fd;

/* Open the file to add to the cache and return a file descriptor. */
fd = open(path, O_RDONLY);

/*
 * If the `open()` command fails, return -1. Remove the corresponding
 * cache entry from the active_cache array if the file does not exist in
 * the working directory.
 */
if (fd < 0) {
    if (errno == ENOENT)
        return remove_file_from_cache(path);
    return -1;
}

/*
 * Get file information and store it in the `st` stat structure. If
 * fstat() fails, release the file descriptor and return -1.
 */
if (fstat(fd, &st) < 0) {
    close(fd);
    return -1;
}

/* Get the length of the file path string. */
namelen = strlen(path);
/* Calculate the size to allocate to the cache entry in bytes. */
size = cache_entry_size(namelen);
/* Allocate `size` bytes to the cache entry. */
ce = malloc(size);
/* Initialize the cache entry to contain null characters. */
memset(ce, 0, size);
```

```
535 /* Copy `path` into the cache entry's `name` member. */
536 memcpy(ce->name, path, namelen);
537
538 /*
539  * Copy the file metadata obtained through the fstat() call to the cache
540  * entry structure members.
541  */
542 ce->ctime.sec = STAT_TIME_SEC( &st, st_ctim );
543 ce->ctime.nsec = STAT_TIME_NSEC( &st, st_ctim );
544 ce->mtime.sec = STAT_TIME_SEC( &st, st_mtim );
545 ce->mtime.nsec = STAT_TIME_NSEC( &st, st_mtim );
546 ce->st_dev = st.st_dev;
547 ce->st_ino = st.st_ino;
548 ce->st_mode = st.st_mode;
549 ce->st_uid = st.st_uid;
550 ce->st_gid = st.st_gid;
551 ce->st_size = st.st_size;
552 ce->namelen = namelen;
```

In lines 542 to 551, data from the `st` stat structure is used to populate the corresponding members in the `ce` `cache_entry` structure. In lines 542 to 545, `STAT_TIME_SEC` is a macro defined in `cache.h` that accommodates the different conventions in different operating systems for naming the status change time and modification time in the stat structure.

8.3 index_fd

Synopsis

```
char *path = argv[1];
struct stat st;
int fd = open(path, O_RDONLY);
fstat(fd, &st);
int namelen = strlen(path);

int size = cache_entry_size(namelen);
struct cache_entry *ce;
ce = malloc(size);
```

```
memset(ce, 0, size);
memcpy(ce->name, path, namelen);

index_fd(path, namelen, ce, fd, &st);
```

Description

The **index_fd** function constructs a blob object corresponding to a file to be added to or updated in the repository, deflates the blob object, calculates the SHA-1 hash of the deflated blob object, then writes the deflated blob object to the object database.

Function prototype

```
static int index_fd(const char *path, int namelen, struct cache_entry *ce,
                    int fd, struct stat *st);
```

Algorithm

The **index_fd** function first maps to memory the contents of the file to be added to or updated in the repository using the **mmap** function. It then constructs the blob object metadata consisting of the string blob and a string containing the decimal form of the size of the file. This metadata is deflated using zlib library functions. The blob object data, consisting of the file contents, is then deflated. The final deflated object is thus a complete deflated blob object that consists of the blob object metadata and data.

The SHA-1 hash of the deflated blob object is then calculated using OpenSSL library functions. Finally, the deflated blob object is written to the object database using the **write_sha1_buffer** function. See Chapter 6 for details of this function.

Return value

On success, **index_fd** returns the return value of the **write_sha1_buffer** function. On failure, it returns -1.

Code snippets

Line 394 maps a file's contents to memory:

```
394 void *in = mmap(NULL, st->st_size, PROT_READ, MAP_PRIVATE, fd, 0);
```

Here, **fd** is the file descriptor for the file to be added to or updated in the repository and **st->size** is the size of that file, which will be the amount of data to map to memory. The **mmap** function returns a pointer to the memory location and this is stored in the in pointer. The **PROT_READ** flag indicates that the memory can be read, and the **MAP_PRIVATE** flag indicates that changes to the mapped data should not be written back to the file.

Here is the part of the **index_fd** function that constructs the blob object and deflates it:

```
420 /* Initialize the zlib stream to contain null characters. */
421 memset(&stream, 0, sizeof(stream));
422
423 /*
424  * Initialize the compression stream for optimized compression
425  * (as opposed to speed).
426  */
427 deflateInit(&stream, Z_BEST_COMPRESSION);
428
429 /*
430  * Linus Torvalds: ASCII size + nul byte
431  */
432 stream.next_in = metadata;    /* Set file metadata as the first addition */
433                               /* to the compression stream input. */
434 /*
435  * Write `blob ` to the `metadata` array, followed by the size of the
436  * file being added to the cache.  Set the number of bytes available as
437  * input for the next compression equal to the number of characters
```

```
438  * written + 1 (for the terminating null character).
439  */
440 stream.avail_in = 1 + sprintf(metadata, "blob %lu",
441                               (unsigned long) st->st_size);
442 /* Specify `out` as the location to write the next compressed output. */
443 stream.next_out = out;
444 /* Number of bytes available for storing the next compressed output. */
445 stream.avail_out = max_out_bytes;
446
447 /* Compress the data, which so far is just the file metadata. */
448 while (deflate(&stream, 0) == Z_OK)
449     /* Linus Torvalds: nothing */;
450
451 /* Add the file content to the compression stream input. */
452 stream.next_in = in;
453 stream.avail_in = st->st_size;
454
455 /* Compress the file content. */
456 while (deflate(&stream, Z_FINISH) == Z_OK)
457     /* Linus Torvalds: nothing */;
458
459 /* Free data structures that were used for compression. */
460 deflateEnd(&stream);
```

A blob object consists of metadata and data, the latter consisting of the corresponding file's contents. In this case, the metadata consists of the blob object tag and the corresponding file's size in bytes, written as a string. This metadata is compressed in lines 440 to 449. The file contents are then compressed in lines 452 to 460. The procedure for compression using the zlib library is similar to that in the `write_sha1_file` function in the `read-cache.c` source file. Please see Chapter 6 for details.

After the blob object is deflated, the SHA-1 hash is calculated:

```
461 /* Initialize the `c` SHA context structure. */
462 SHA1_Init(&c);
463 /*
464  * Calculate the hash of the compressed output, which has total size
465  * `stream.total_out`.
466  */
467 SHA1_Update(&c, out, stream.total_out);
468 /*
```

```
469  * Store the SHA1 hash of the compressed output in the cache entry's
470  * `sha1` member.
471  */
472 SHA1_Final(ce->sha1, &c);
```

Again, this procedure is similar to that found in the **write_sha1_file** function in the **read-cache.c** source file. In line 472, the SHA-1 hash of the deflated blob object is stored in the cache entry structure's **sha1** member.

Finally, the deflated blob object is written to the object database using the **write_sha1_buffer** function that was discussed in Chapter 6:

```
/*
 * Write the blob object to the object store and return with the return
 * value of the write_sha1_buffer function.
 */
return write_sha1_buffer(ce->sha1, out, stream.total_out);
```

8.4 add_cache_entry

Synopsis

```
struct cache_entry *ce;
...
add_cache_entry(ce);
```

Description

The **add_cache_entry** function inserts a cache entry into the **active_cache** array lexicographically.

Function prototype

```
static int add_cache_entry(struct cache_entry *ce);
```

Algorithm

The **add_cache_entry** function first calls the **cache_name_pos** function to get the index where the current cache entry will be inserted in the **active_cache** array. If a cache entry with the same path as the current cache entry already exists, then that cache entry is replaced with the current cache entry.

The function then checks if there is enough space in the **active_cache** array to insert the current cache entry. If not, then the maximum number of elements allocated to the array is increased.

The global variable **active_nr,** which keeps track of the number of cache entries, is then incremented and the current cache entry is inserted into the **active_cache** array using the **memmove** function.

Return value

The **add_cache_entry** function returns a value of 0.

Code snippets

Here is this short function in its entirety:

```
static int add_cache_entry(struct cache_entry *ce)
{
    /*
     * Get the index where the cache entry will be inserted in the
     * active_cache array.
     */
    int pos;
    pos = cache_name_pos(ce->name, ce->namelen);

```

```
343     /* Linus Torvalds: existing match? Just replace it */
344     if (pos < 0) {
345         active_cache[-pos-1] = ce;
346         return 0;
347     }
348 
349     /*
350      * Make sure the `active_cache` array has space for the additional cache
351      * entry.
352      */
353     if (active_nr == active_alloc) {
354         active_alloc = alloc_nr(active_alloc);
355         active_cache = realloc(active_cache,
356                                active_alloc * sizeof(struct cache_entry *));
357     }
358 
359     /* Insert the new cache entry into the active_cache array. */
360     active_nr++;
361     if (active_nr > pos)
362         memmove(active_cache + pos + 1, active_cache + pos,
363                 (active_nr - pos - 1) * sizeof(ce));
364     active_cache[pos] = ce;
365     return 0;
366 }
```

Line 341 calls the **cache_name_pos** function, which does a binary search to determine the index **pos** in the **active_cache** array where the cache entry of the file with path **ce->name** will be inserted lexicographically.

Line 353 checks if the **active_cache** array is full. If it is, then the **realloc** function is called in line 355 to increase the size of the **active_cache** array.

In line 360, the global variable **active_nr** is incremented to reflect the addition of a new cache entry in the **active_cache** array. Finally, the new cache entry is inserted in the **active_cache** array in lines 361 to 364 using the **pos** index. The **memmove** function is used in lines 362 and 363 to move cache entries in the **active_cache** array to make way for the new cache entry to be inserted.

8.5 write_cache

Synopsis

```
int newfd;
...
write_cache(newfd, active_cache, active_nr);
```

Description

The `write_cache` function writes the cache header and the cache entries in the `active_cache` array to the `.dircache/index.lock` file.

Function prototype

```
static int write_cache(int newfd, struct cache_entry **cache, int entries);
```

Algorithm

The `write_cache` function first stores the cache signature, version, and the number of cache entries in the `active_cache` array in the cache header structure. Then it calculates the SHA-1 hash value of the cache header and each of the cache entries in the `active_cache` array. This hash value is then stored in the header structure, and then the resulting cache (header and cache entries) is written to the `.dircache/index.lock` file.

Return value

On success, `write_cache` returns 0. On failure, it returns -1;

Code snippets

Here is the entirety of this short function:

```c
static int write_cache(int newfd, struct cache_entry **cache, int entries)
{
    SHA_CTX c;                  /* Declare an SHA context structure. */
    struct cache_header hdr;    /* Declare a cache_header structure. */
    int i;                      /* For loop iterator. */

    /* Set this to the signature defined in "cache.h". */
    hdr.signature = CACHE_SIGNATURE;
    /* The version is always set to 1 in this release. */
    hdr.version = 1;
    /*
     * Store the number of cache entries in the `active_cache` array in the
     * cache header.
     */
    hdr.entries = entries;

    /* Initialize the `c` SHA context structure. */
    SHA1_Init(&c);
    /* Update the running SHA1 hash calculation with the cache header. */
    SHA1_Update(&c, &hdr, offsetof(struct cache_header, sha1));
    /* Update the running SHA1 hash calculation with each cache entry. */
    for (i = 0; i < entries; i++) {
        struct cache_entry *ce = cache[i];
        int size = ce_size(ce);
        SHA1_Update(&c, ce, size);
    }
    /* Store the final SHA1 hash in the header. */
    SHA1_Final(hdr.sha1, &c);

    /* Write the cache header to the index lock file. */
    if (write(newfd, &hdr, sizeof(hdr)) != sizeof(hdr))
        return -1;

    /* Write each of the cache entries to the index lock file. */
    for (i = 0; i < entries; i++) {
        struct cache_entry *ce = cache[i];
        int size = ce_size(ce);
        if (write(newfd, ce, size) != size)
            return -1;
    }
    return 0;
}
```

The cache header is constructed in lines 587 to 594. The SHA-1 hash of the cache header and of the cache entries is calculated in lines 597 to 605. The final hash value of the entire cache is stored in the header structure member `sha1` in line 607. The calls to the OpenSSL library functions are similar to those discussed in Chapter 6.

Finally, the cache header and the cache entries are written to the index lock file in lines 610 to 619.

9 write-tree.c

9.1 main

Synopsis

```
write-tree
```

Description

The **write-tree** command writes the information in the cache to a tree object. For each file represented as a cache entry in the cache, the following data are written to a tree object:

```
file mode
file path
SHA-1 hash of deflated blob object
```

Algorithm

The code first calls the **read_cache** function to read the cache entries in the **.dircache/index** cache file into the global **active_cache** array and store the number of cache entries in the **active_nr** global variable.

Using the **malloc** function, memory is allocated to a buffer that will be used for storing tree metadata and data. A buffer index called **offset** is used to index the byte in the buffer that will be written to next. Initially, this is set to **ORIG_OFFSET**, a macro defined in the **write-tree.c** source file. The tree data will be written starting at this offset, and the tree metadata before it.

For each cache entry in the `active_cache` array, the `check_valid_sha1` function is called to check if the cache entry's SHA-1 hash member is valid, i.e. that an object exists in the object database that corresponds to this SHA-1 hash and that this object can be read by the process.

If the SHA-1 hash is valid, the buffer is checked if there is enough space available to add the current cache entry's metadata. If not, then the buffer space is increased using the `realloc` function.

Next, for the current cache entry, the file mode, file path, and SHA-1 hash of the deflated blob object corresponding to the file are written to the buffer, with the `offset` index adjusted at each step to reflect the index of the next buffer byte to write to.

After all the cache entries are processed, the `prepend_integer` function is called to prepend to the tree data a string containing the decimal form of the size of the tree data in bytes. The size of the tree data can be calculated using `offset - ORIG_OFFSET`. The string "tree " is then also prepended to the string containing the tree data size.

The buffer is then adjusted to start at the first character of the "tree" object tag, and the final total size of the buffer is calculated.

Finally, using the `write_sha1_file` function, the buffer is deflated, the SHA-1 hash is calculated, and then the tree object is written to the object database.

Return value

On success, the `main` function returns 0. On failure, it returns 1.

Code snippets

Here is the part of the `main` function that loops through the cache entries to build the tree object:

```
/* Linus Torvalds: Guess at an initial size */
size = entries * 40 + 400;
/* Allocate `size` bytes to buffer to store the tree content. */
buffer = malloc(size);
/*
 * Set the offset index using the macro defined in this file. The tree
 * data will be written starting at this offset.  The tree metadata will
 * be written before it.
 */
offset = ORIG_OFFSET;

/*
 * Loop over each cache entry and build the tree object by adding the
 * data from the cache entry to the buffer.
 */
for (i = 0; i < entries; i++) {
    /* Pick out the ith cache entry from the active_cache array. */
    struct cache_entry *ce = active_cache[i];

    /* Check if the cache entry's SHA1 hash is valid. Otherwise, exit. */
    if (check_valid_sha1(ce->sha1) < 0)
        exit(1);

    /* If needed, increase the size of the buffer. */
    if (offset + ce->namelen + 60 > size) {
        size = alloc_nr(offset + ce->namelen + 60);
        buffer = realloc(buffer, size);
    }

    /*
     * Write the cache entry's file mode and name to the buffer and
     * increment `offset` by the number of characters that were written.
     */
    offset += sprintf(buffer + offset, "%o %s", ce->st_mode, ce->name);

    /*
     * Write a null character to the buffer as a separator and increment
     * `offset`.
     */
    buffer[offset++] = 0;

    /* Add the cache entry's SHA1 hash to the buffer. */
    memcpy(buffer + offset, ce->sha1, 20);

    /*
     * Increment the offset by 20 bytes, the length of an SHA1 hash.
     */
```

```
250    offset += 20;
251 }
```

Line 206 allocates memory to the buffer using the `malloc` function, where the value of `size` is calculated in line 204. The value of `entries` is the number of cache entries in the `active_cache` array. Remember that, for each cache entry, the only data written to the tree are the file mode, the file path, and the blob object's SHA-1 hash, so the amount of memory needed is not very big.

In line 212, the `offset` index is initialized to the value of the `ORIG_OFFSET` macro. The value of this macro can be found in line 161 of the source code and is equal to 40. So 40 bytes at the beginning of the buffer are allocated for the tree metadata – which consists of the tree object tag and the tree data size – and the rest of the buffer is allocated for the tree data.

The tree object data is constructed in lines 218 to 251, where the code loops over the cache entries in the `active_cache` array. The current cache entry's file mode and file path are written to the buffer in line 236. This is followed by a null character in line 242. Finally, the 20-byte SHA-1 hash of the deflated blob object is written to the buffer in line 245 using the `memcpy` function. Notice how the `offset` pointer is incremented by the number of characters written to the buffer in lines 236, 242, and 250.

9.2 prepend_integer

Synopsis

```
char *buffer;
unsigned int offset;
...
prepend_integer(buffer, offset - ORIG_OFFSET, ORIG_OFFSET);
```

Description

The `prepend_integer` function prepends to the tree data in the buffer a string containing the decimal form of the size of the tree data in bytes.

Function prototype

```
static int prepend_integer(char *buffer, unsigned val, int i);
```

Algorithm

The `prepend_integer` function first decrements the buffer index passed as a function argument. In this case, the value of this index is `ORIG_OFFSET` and is stored in the variable `i`. The function then writes a null character to the buffer at the byte specified by the index `i`. This null character serves to separate the tree metadata from the tree data.

The string containing the decimal form of the size of the tree data in bytes is then written to the buffer, starting from the least significant digit. The index `i` is decremented before each character is written to the buffer at the byte indexed by the resulting index.

The function then returns the current value of the index `i`, i.e. the index of the buffer element that contains the most significant digit of the decimal form of the tree data size.

Return value

The `prepend_integer` function returns the current value of the buffer index `i`.

Code snippets

Here is the short function in its entirety:

```
140 static int prepend_integer(char *buffer, unsigned val, int i)
141 {
142     /* Prepend a null character to the tree data in the buffer. */
143     buffer[--i] = '\0';
144 
145     /*
146      * Prepend a string containing the decimal form of the size of the tree
147      * data in bytes before the null character.
148      */
149     do {
150         buffer[--i] = '0' + (val % 10);
151         val /= 10;
152     } while (val);
153     /*
154      * The value of `i` is now the index of the buffer element that contains
155      * the most significant digit of the decimal form of the tree data size.
156      */
157     return i;
158 }
159 
160 /* Linus Torvalds: Enough space to add the header of "tree <size>\0" */
161 #define ORIG_OFFSET (40)
```

The string containing the decimal form of the size of the tree data is constructed in lines 149 to 152. The size of the tree data is stored in the variable `val`, which is passed as a function argument. The expression `(val % 10)` in line 150 is equal to the remainder after dividing `val` by 10. The corresponding ASCII character is then written to the buffer after the index `i` is decremented. In effect, this writes the character corresponding to the least significant digit of the decimal form of `val` in the buffer at the current index.

The expression `val /= 10` in line 151 is an integer division, so the fractional part of the quotient is discarded. Again, the character corresponding to the least significant digit of the resulting `val` is written in the buffer in line 150 after the index `i` is decremented.

This loop continues until all digits of the decimal form of `val` are written to the buffer. In line 157, the current value of the index `i` is returned to the calling function. This value is the index of the buffer element that contains the most significant digit of the decimal form of `val` since this was the last character written to the buffer.

Finally, note the definition of the `ORIG_OFFSET` macro in line 161.

10 commit-tree.c

In this chapter, we discuss the more salient functions in the `commit-tree.c` source code.

10.1 main

Synopsis

```
commit-tree <tree hash> [(-p <parent hash>)...] < changelog
```

Description

This command creates a commit object for the specified tree object and then saves the commit object to the object database. It also optionally takes as input the SHA-1 hash values of parent commit objects. It expects a text file that contains the user comment - today known as the commit message - for the commit to be specified using the < redirection operator.

Algorithm

The `main` function first checks if each hash given in the command line for the tree and parent commit objects, if any, is a valid 40-character hexadecimal representation of an SHA-1 hash value. Next, it gets the user or author credentials and the hostname and constructs an email address using these. It then gets the current calendar time and converts it to a human-readable string containing the corresponding local date and time.

It then checks if the following environment variables are defined: `COMMITTER_NAME, COMMITER_EMAIL, COMMITER_DATE`. If an environment variable is defined, then that value is used in the commit object for the corresponding committer field. Otherwise, the same value that was previously obtained for the user or author is used. Special characters are then removed from the strings containing the author and committer name, email, and commit date and time.

Next, it calls the `init_buffer` function to allocate memory to and initialize a buffer where the commit object metadata and data will be stored. The first `ORIG_OFFSET` bytes of this buffer are initialized to contain the null character. As with the `write-tree` command, this `ORIG_OFFSET` macro is defined as 40 in the source code, and the first 40 bytes of the buffer is allocated for the object metadata.

It then calls the `add_buffer` function to write to the buffer each of following items, which comprise the commit object data:

```
tree object SHA-1 hash value
SHA-1 hash values of parent commit objects
author name, email, and commit date
committer name, email, and commit date
user comment
```

The `finish_buffer` command is then called to prepend the commit object metadata to the commit object data, namely:

```
the "commit" object tag
a string containing the decimal form of the size of the commit data
```

Finally, the `write_sha1_file` function is called to deflate the buffer, calculate the SHA-1 hash value, and write the commit object to the object database, using its hash as an index.

Return value

On success, the `main` function returns 0. On failure, it returns 1.

Code snippets

Here is the part of the **main** function that uses the **add_buffer** function to add the commit object data to the buffer:

```
/* Add the string 'tree ' and the tree SHA1 hash to the buffer. */
add_buffer(&buffer, &size, "tree %s\n", sha1_to_hex(tree_sha1));

/*
 * For each parent commit SHA1 hash, add the string 'parent ' and the
 * hash to the buffer.
 *
 * Linus Torvalds: NOTE! This ordering means that the same exact tree
 * merged with a * different order of parents will be a _different_
 * changeset even if everything else stays the same.
 */
for (i = 0; i < parents; i++)
    add_buffer(&buffer, &size, "parent %s\n",
               sha1_to_hex(parent_sha1[i]));

/*
 * Add the author and committer name, email, and commit time to the
 * buffer.
 */
add_buffer(&buffer, &size, "author %s <%s> %s\n", gecos, email, date);
add_buffer(&buffer, &size, "committer %s <%s> %s\n\n",
           realgecos, realemail, realdate);
/*
 * Add the commit message to the buffer. This is what requires the user to
 * type CTRL-D to finish the `commit-tree` command.
 */
while (fgets(comment, sizeof(comment), stdin) != NULL)
    add_buffer(&buffer, &size, "%s", comment);
```

One can see that the **add_buffer** function takes a variable argument list after the format string. This makes it a flexible function for writing to the buffer the different items that comprise the commit object data.

Note that the **size** variable, which is the size of the filled portion of the buffer, is updated with the current size each time the **add_buffer** function is called. See the next section for a discussion of the **add_buffer** function.

10.2 add_buffer

Synopsis

```
unsigned char tree_sha1[20];
char *buffer;
unsigned int size;
...
get_sha1_hex(argv[1], tree_sha1);
add_buffer(&buffer, &size, "tree %s\n", sha1_to_hex(tree_sha1));
```

Description

The **add_buffer** function adds one item of commit object data to the buffer.

Function prototype

```
static void add_buffer(char **bufp, unsigned int *sizep, const char *fmt, ...);
```

Algorithm

The **add_buffer** function takes a variable argument list, so it can be used to format and add a variety of strings to the buffer. In the function definition, the named arguments are **bufp**, which is a pointer to a pointer to the commit object buffer, **sizep** which is a pointer to the size of the filled portion of the buffer, and **fmt**, which is a formatted string to be written to the buffer. The unnamed arguments come after the **fmt** string.

The **add_buffer** function first calls the **va_start** function to initialize the **args** **va_list** variable to point to the first unnamed argument after the **fmt** string. The **vsnprintf** function is then called to construct the **fmt** string using the **args** variable argument list object, and then write the string to the **one_line** character array.

The length of the string that was written by **vsnprintf** is returned and stored in **len**. The **va_end** function is then called to clean up the **args** variable argument list object.

The value in **len** is added to the current size of the filled portion of the buffer to obtain the expected size, **newsize**, of the filled portion of the buffer after the current string in **one_line** is added to it. If this is larger than the current maximum buffer size, then the buffer size is increased using the **realloc** function. Note that the maximum size allocated to the buffer is always a multiple of 32,768 bytes.

Finally, ***sizep** is updated to **newsize** and the string in **one_line** is copied to the buffer using the **memcpy** function.

Return value

The **add_buffer** function has return type **void** and has no return value.

Code snippets

Here is the part of the **add_buffer** function that uses a variable argument list to form the string to be added to the buffer:

```
/* Initialize args to point to the first unnamed argument after fmt. */
va_start(args, fmt);

/*
 * Use variable argument list args to construct the fmt string and write
 * the string to one_line.
 */
len = vsnprintf(one_line, sizeof(one_line), fmt, args);
```

```
230 /* Clean up args variable list object. */
231 va_end(args);
```

Line 222 initializes the **args va_list** object to point to the first unnamed argument after the **fmt** format string. The **fmt** string is constructed using the **args** object and written to **one_line** in line 228.

Here is the part of the function that checks the buffer size and writes the string in **one_line** to the buffer:

```
232     /* Current size of filled portion of commit object buffer. */
233     size = *sizep;
234     /* Add length of one_line to the size of the filled buffer portion. */
235     newsize = size + len;
236     /*
237      * Calculate the current maximum buffer size. Should be a multiple of
238      * 32768 bytes.
239      */
240     alloc = (size + 32767) & ~32767;
241     /* Set local pointer to point to the commit object buffer. */
242     buf = *bufp;
243 
244     /*
245      * Increase the buffer size if the expected size of the filled portion of
246      * the buffer is greater than the calculated maximum buffer size.
247      */
248     if (newsize > alloc) {
249         /*
250          * Calculate new maximum buffer size. Should be a multiple of 32768
251          * bytes.
252          */
253         alloc = (newsize + 32767) & ~32767;
254         /* Increase the buffer size. */
255         buf = realloc(buf, alloc);
256         /* Set the commit object buffer to the reallocated buffer. */
257         *bufp = buf;
258     }
259     /* New size of filled portion of commit object buffer. */
260     *sizep = newsize;
261     /*
262      * Append one_line after the filled portion of the commit object
263      * buffer.
264      */
265     memcpy(buf + size, one_line, len);
```

```
266 }
```

Line 235 adds the length of the string in **one_line** to the current size of the filled portion of the buffer, size, and stores this new size to **newsize**. The current maximum buffer size is calculated in line 240 using size and stored in **alloc**. Note that the maximum buffer size is a multiple of 32,768 bytes.

Line 248 checks if the buffer has enough space to accommodate the new string that will be added. If not, a new maximum buffer size is calculated in line 253 using newsize, and the buffer size is increased in line 255 using the **realloc** function.

Finally ***sizep** is updated with the expected size of the filled portion of the buffer (line 260), and the string in **one_line** is written to the buffer beginning at the index **size** (line 265), which is the current size of the filled portion of the buffer (see line 233).

10.3 finish_buffer

Synopsis

```
char *buffer;
unsigned int size;
...
finish_buffer("commit ", &buffer, &size);
```

Description

The **finish_buffer** function prepends to the commit object data a string containing the decimal form of the size of the commit object data in bytes, and then prepends the commit object tag to this.

Function prototype

```
static void finish_buffer(char *tag, char **bufp, unsigned int *sizep);
```

Algorithm

The **finish_buffer** function first calls the **prepend_integer** function to prepend to the commit object data a string containing the decimal form of the size of the commit object data in bytes. The **prepend_integer** function is a static function and is exactly the same as that found in the **write-tree.c** source file. See Chapter 9 for details of the **prepend_integer** function.

The final size of the filled portion of the buffer is then calculated and the string "commit " is prepended to the string containing the commit data size to identify the object as a commit object. Finally, the buffer is adjusted so it starts at the first character of the "commit" object tag.

Return value

The **finish_buffer** function has return type **void** and has no return value.

Code snippets

Here is the entirety of this short function:

```
static void finish_buffer(char *tag, char **bufp, unsigned int *sizep)
{
    /* The length of the string containing the object tag. */
    int taglen;
    /* Index of the element of the buffer to be filled next. */
    int offset;
    /* Set local pointer to point to the commit object buffer. */
    char *buf = *bufp;
    /* Current size of filled portion of commit object buffer. */
```

```
317     unsigned int size = *sizep;
318
319     /* Prepend the size of the commit object data in bytes to the buffer. */
320     offset = prepend_integer(buf, size - ORIG_OFFSET, ORIG_OFFSET);
321     /* Get the length of the string containing the object tag. */
322     taglen = strlen(tag);
323     /* Decrement offset index by length of the object tag string. */
324     offset -= taglen;
325     /*
326      * Point to the byte in the buffer where the first character of the object
327      * tag string will be written.
328      */
329     buf += offset;
330     /*
331      * Calculate final size of filled portion of buffer, i.e., the size of the
332      * commit object.
333      */
334     size -= offset;
335     /* Prepend the string with commit object tag to the buffer. */
336     memcpy(buf, tag, taglen);
337
338     /*
339      * Adjust buffer to start at the first character of the `commit` object
340      * tag.
341      */
342     *bufp = buf;
343
344     /* Final size of the commit object. */
345     *sizep = size;
346 }
```

Line 315 sets a local pointer to point to the commit object buffer. The **prepend_integer** function is called in line 320 to prepend to the commit object data a string containing the decimal form of the size of the commit object data in bytes. This function returns the index of the buffer element containing the most significant digit of the size, and this is stored in the **offset** index.

In line 324, this index is decremented by the length of the string containing the commit object tag. In line 329, the local **buffer** pointer, initially pointing to element 0, is updated to point to the element of the buffer at **offset** index. This is the starting byte of the part of the buffer where **tag**, the string containing the commit object tag, is written. This is done in line 336 using the **memcpy** function.

The final size of the filled portion of the buffer is calculated in line 334. In line 342, the buffer is adjusted to start at the first character of the "commit" object tag. Finally `*sizep` is updated with the final size of the filled portion of the buffer in line 345.

11 read-tree.c

The `read-tree.c` source file is short and consists of only two functions, both of which we will discuss in this chapter.

11.1 main

Synopsis

```
read-tree <tree hash>
```

Description

The `read-tree` command reads a tree object from the object database and displays on screen the file mode, file path, and SHA-1 hash of each blob object represented in the tree.

Algorithm

The `main` function first converts the 40-character hexadecimal SHA-1 hash specified by the user on the command line to its equivalent 20-byte representation. It then checks if the `SHA1_FILE_DIRECTORY` environment variable is defined. If defined, then the value of that environment variable is used as the path of the object database.

The `unpack` function is then called to read and inflate the specified tree object via the `read_sha1_file` function, and then to write to standard output the metadata for each blob object represented in the tree.

Return value

On success, the `main` function returns 0. On failure, it returns 1.

Code snippets

Here is the entirety of the short and straightforward **main** function:

```
int main(int argc, char **argv)
{
    /* A file descriptor. */
    int fd;
    /* String to hold the 20-byte representation of a hash value. */
    unsigned char sha1[20];

    /*
     * Validate the number of command line arguments, which should be equal to
     * 2 since the command itself is also counted. If not, print a usage
     * message and exit.
     */
    if (argc != 2)
        usage("read-tree <key>");

    /*
     * Convert the given 40-character hexadecimal representation of an SHA1
     * hash value to the equivalent 20-byte representation. If conversion
     * fails (for example, if the hexadecimal representation has a character
     * outside the valid hexadecimal range of 0-9, a-f, or A-F), print usage
     * message and exit.
     */
    if (get_sha1_hex(argv[1], sha1) < 0)
        usage("read-tree <key>");

    /*
     * Set `sha1_file_directory` (i.e. the path to the object store) to the
     * value of the `DB_ENVIRONMENT` environment variable, which defaults to
     * `SHA1_FILE_DIRECTORY` as defined in "cache.h". If the environment
     * variable is not set (and it most likely won't be), getenv() will return
     * a null pointer.
     */
    sha1_file_directory = getenv(DB_ENVIRONMENT);

    /*
     * If object store path was not set from the environment variable above,
     * set it to the default value, `.dircache/objects`, the definition of the
     * token `DEFAULT_DB_ENVIRONMENT` in "cache.h".
     */
    if (!sha1_file_directory)
        sha1_file_directory = DEFAULT_DB_ENVIRONMENT;

    /*
     * Call `unpack()` function with the binary SHA1 hash of the tree object
```

```
230      * as the function parameter.
231      */
232     if (unpack(sha1) < 0)
233         usage("unpack failed");
234
235     return 0;
236 }
```

The SHA-1 hash value is converted from a 40-character hexadecimal representation to the equivalent 20-byte representation in line 208.

In line 218, the path to the object database is then set to the value of the `SHA1_FILE_DIRECTORY` environment variable. If the `SHA1_FILE_DIRECTORY` environment variable is not defined, then the default object database path, `.dircache/objects`, is used in line 226.

Finally, the `unpack` function is called in line 232 to read and inflate the specified tree object and to print to screen the tree object data.

11.2 unpack

Synopsis

```
unsigned char sha1[20];
get_sha1_hex(argv[1], sha1);
unpack(sha1);
```

Description

The `unpack` function calls the `read_sha1_file` function to read and inflate a tree object from the object store, and then prints the tree data to standard output.

Function prototype

```
static int unpack(unsigned char *sha1);
```

Algorithm

The unpack function first calls the read_sha1_file function to read and inflate a tree object from the object store and to return a pointer to the buffer containing the tree object data without the prepended tree object metadata. The tree object's type and data size are returned in the type and size variables respectively. The object type is then checked to make sure the object is a tree object. If it is not, an error message is displayed and the unpack function exits.

For each blob object represented in the tree object, the unpack function then reads from the buffer the blob object's SHA-1 hash value and the path and the mode of the file corresponding to the blob object. To do this, the unpack function uses the fact that a null character and a space are used to delimit these three pieces of metadata. This metadata is then displayed on the screen.

Return value

On success, the unpack function returns 0. On failure, it returns 1.

Code snippets

Here is the part of the unpack function that loops through the blob objects represented in the tree object:

```
/*
 * Read metadata about each blob object from the tree object data buffer.
 */
while (size) {
    /* Calculate offset to the current blob object's SHA1 hash. */
```

```
    int len = strlen(buffer) + 1;
    /* Point to the current blob object's SHA1 hash. */
    unsigned char *sha1 = buffer + len;
    /*
     * Point to the path of the file corresponding to the current blob
     * object.
     */
    char *path = strchr(buffer, ' ') + 1;
    unsigned int mode;

    /*
     * Verify the current size of the buffer and get the mode of the file
     * corresponding to the current blob object. If either fails, display
     * error message then exit.
     */
    if (size < len + 20 || sscanf(buffer, "%o", &mode) != 1)
        usage("corrupt 'tree' file");

    /*
     * Adjust buffer to point to the start of the next blob object's
     * metadata.
     */
    buffer = sha1 + 20;
    /*
     * Decrement size by the length of the metadata that was read for the
     * current blob object.
     */
    size -= len + 20;

    /*
     * Display the mode and path of the file corresponding to the current
     * blob object, and the 40-character representation of the current
     * blob object's SHA1 hash.
     */
    printf("%o %s (%s)\n", mode, path, sha1_to_hex(sha1));
}
```

This while loop reads the tree data in the buffer until `size`, which keeps track of the amount of tree data left to read, is equal to 0, i.e. all the tree data has been read.

In order to understand this piece of code, it is useful to recall the structure of a tree object:

```
"tree"              (tree object tag)
' '                 (single space)
size of tree data (in bytes)
'\0'                (null character)
file 1 mode         (octal number)
' '
file 1 path
'\0'
blob 1 SHA-1 hash (hash of deflated blob)
file 2 mode
' '
file 2 path
'\0'
blob 2 SHA-1 hash
...
file N mode
' '
file N path
'\0'
blob N SHA-1 hash
```

Note that a space separates each file's mode and path, while a null character separates the corresponding blob's SHA-1 hash from the file path.

Line 135 calculates the offset to the current blob object's SHA-1 hash. The `strlen` function returns the number of characters in the buffer until it encounters a null character. The `+ 1` expression is there to take into account the null character itself in the length. Thus, `len` points to the element in the buffer where the current blob object's SHA-1 value starts. Line 137 points `sha1` to that element, effectively reading the SHA-1 hash of the current object.

Line 142 reads from the buffer the path of the file corresponding to the current blob object. The `strchr` function returns a pointer to the first occurrence of a space in the buffer. The `+ 1`, again, is there to skip the space itself.

In line 157, the buffer is adjusted so that it points to the first byte after the current SHA-1 hash, i.e. so that it points to the start of the next blob object represented in the tree. The size of the buffer is correspondingly decreased by the number of bytes read for the current blob object (line 162). Finally, the file mode and path and the blob object's SHA-1 hash are printed to screen in line 169.

12 cat-file.c

12.1 main

Synopsis

```
cat-file <object hash>
```

where the object is either a blob object or a commit object.

Description

This command reads a blob or commit object and writes the inflated object data to a uniquely named temporary text file.

NOTE	When reading a tree object, the `read-tree` command should be used instead.

Algorithm

The code first checks if there are 2 command line arguments and converts the specified 40-character hexadecimal hash to the equivalent 20-byte representation. If either one fails, a usage message is displayed on the screen and the code terminates execution.

Otherwise, it calls the `read_sha1_file` function to read and inflate the object with the specified SHA-1 hash from the object store and return a pointer to a buffer that contains the inflated object data.

The code then uses the `mkstemp` function to create and open a text file whose name is unique and has the template `temp_git_file_XXXXXX`, where `XXXXXX` is a string randomly generated by `mkstemp`. The buffer containing the object data is then written to this text file, and the filename and object type are then printed out to screen.

Return value

On failure, the `cat-file` command returns 1.

Code snippets

The `cat-file.c` source file is short, straightforward, and consists only of the `main` function. Here is the portion of the code that reads the object from the object database and writes the inflated object data to an output file with a unique filename:

```
/*
 * Read the object whose SHA1 hash is `sha1` from the object store,
 * inflate it, and return a pointer to the object data (without the
 * prepended metadata). Store the object type and object data size in
 * `type` and `size` respectively.
 */
buf = read_sha1_file(sha1, type, &size);

/*
 * Exit if `buf` is a null pointer, i.e., if reading the object from the
 * object store failed.
 */
if (!buf)
    exit(1);

/*
 * Modify `template` to generate a unique filename, then open the file for
 * reading and writing and return a file descriptor for the file. The
 * `XXXXXX` in the template is replaced with a randomly generated
 * alphanumeric string to generate a unique filename.
 */
fd = mkstemp(template);

/* If mkstemp() fails, print error message and exit. */
if (fd < 0)
    usage("unable to create tempfile");

/*
```

```
156  * Write the object data, which has length `size` bytes, to the output
157  * file associated with `fd`. If the number of bytes written does not
158  * equal the object data size, then set object `type` to "bad".
159  */
160 if (write(fd, buf, size) != size)
161     strcpy(type, "bad");
162
163 /* Print the output filename and object type to screen. */
164 printf("%s: %s\n", template, type);
```

The filename template is defined in line 115:

```
114 /* A template string used to generate a unique output filename. */
115 char template[] = "temp_git_file_XXXXXX";
```

Line 149 calls the **mkstemp** function to generate a unique filename with this template and opens that file for reading and writing. It returns a file descriptor that's stored in **fd**. Line 160 writes the inflated object data that's in the buffer to this file. The filename and object type is then printed to the screen in line 164.

13 show-diff.c

In this chapter, we will discuss the three functions that comprise the `show-diff.c` source file.

13.1 main

Synopsis

```
show-diff
```

Description

For each entry in the cache, the `show-diff` command prints out the differences between the blob object data and the contents of the corresponding working file. If no differences are found then the `show-diff` command outputs the file path followed by the string "ok".

If differences are found, then the code prints out the file path and the hexadecimal representation of the SHA-1 hash of the blob object, followed by the differences that are output by the `diff` command.

Algorithm

The `main` function first calls the `read_cache` function to read the cache entries into the `active_cache` array and then return the number of cache entries.

For each cache entry in the `active_cache` array, the `stat` function is called to obtain the metadata of the corresponding working file and store it in a `stat` structure. The `match_stat` function is then called to compare the metadata stored in the cache entry to the metadata of the working file stored in the `stat` structure to check if there have been changes.

If none of the metadata changed, then the code prints out the file path and the string "ok", and then the next cache entry is checked.

If any of the metadata changed, then the code prints out the file path and the hexadecimal representation of the SHA-1 hash of the blob object corresponding to the cache entry. The code then calls the `read_sha1_file` function to read and inflate the blob object from the object store and then return a pointer to a buffer that contains the inflated object data. The code then calls the `show_differences` function to print out the differences between the buffer contents and the contents of the working file that corresponds to the current cache entry.

Return value

On success, the `show-diff` command returns 0. On failure, it returns 1.

Code snippets

Here is the part of the `main` function that checks for and displays differences in the metadata and blob data of a cache entry and those of the corresponding working file:

```
/*
 * Compare the metadata stored in the cache entry to those of the
 * corresponding working file to check if they are the same or if
 * anything changed.
 */
changed = match_stat(ce, &st);

/*
 * If no metadata changed, display an ok message and continue to the
 * next cache entry in the active_cache array.
 */
```

```
240 if (!changed) {
241     printf("%s: ok\n", ce->name);
242     continue;
243 }
244
245 /* Fall through here if any metadata changed. */
246
247 /*
248  * Display the path of the file corresponding to the current cache
249  * entry.
250  */
251 printf("%.*s:  ", ce->namelen, ce->name);
252
253 /*
254  * Display the hexadecimal representation of the SHA1 hash of the blob
255  * object corresponding to the current cache entry.
256  */
257 for (n = 0; n < 20; n++)
258     printf("%02x", ce->sha1[n]);
259
260 printf("\n");    /* Print a newline. */
261
262 /*
263  * Read the blob object from the object store using its SHA1 hash,
264  * inflate it, and return a pointer to the object data (without the
265  * prepended metadata). Store the object type and object data size in
266  * `type` and `size` respectively.
267  */
268 new = read_sha1_file(ce->sha1, type, &size);
269
270 /*
271  * Use the diff shell command to display the differences between the
272  * blob data corresponding to the current cache entry and the contents
273  * of the corresponding working file.
274  */
275 show_differences(ce, &st, new, size);
```

Line 234 is where the **match_stat** function is called to compare the metadata stored in the cache entry to those of the corresponding working file. Line 240 checks if there were no changes in the metadata.

If there were changes in the metadata, then the path of the file represented in the current cache entry is printed out in line 251, and the hexadecimal representation of the SHA-1 hash of the corresponding blob object is printed out in lines 257 and 258.

The inflated blob object data is then read into a buffer in line 268, and the **show_differences** function is called in line 275 to compare the blob object data to the contents of the corresponding working file.

13.2 match_stat

Synopsis

```
struct cache_entry *ce;
struct stat st;
int changed;
...
stat(ce->name, &st);
changed = match_stat(ce, &st);
```

Description

The **match_stat** function compares the metadata stored in a cache entry to the metadata of the corresponding working file to check if they are the same or if anything changed.

Function prototype

```
static int match_stat(struct cache_entry *ce, struct stat *st);
```

Algorithm

The **match_stat** function first initializes the flag changed to the default value of 0, indicating that there are no changes in the metadata stored in the current cache entry compared to the metadata of the corresponding working file.

The following file metadata are then compared:

```
time of file's last modification
time of file's last status change
file user ID
file group ID
file mode (type and permissions)
device ID of device containing the file
file inode number
file size
```

If any of these metadata changed then the changed flag is set to indicate which of the metadata changed. Each kind of change results in the corresponding bit being set in the changed flag. This flag is then returned to the `main` function.

Return value

The `match_stat` function returns the value of the changed flag.

Code snippets

Here is the entirety of the short `match_stat` function:

```
static int match_stat(struct cache_entry *ce, struct stat *st)
{
    /* Flag to indicate which file metadata changed, if any. */
    unsigned int changed = 0;

    /*
     * Compare metadata stored in a cache entry to those of the corresponding
     * working file to check if they are the same.
     */

    /* Check last modification time. */
```

```
    if (ce->mtime.sec  != (unsigned int)STAT_TIME_SEC( st, st_mtim ) ||
        ce->mtime.nsec != (unsigned int)STAT_TIME_NSEC( st, st_mtim ))
            changed |= MTIME_CHANGED;
    /* Check time of last status change. */
    if (ce->ctime.sec  != (unsigned int)STAT_TIME_SEC( st, st_ctim ) ||
        ce->ctime.nsec != (unsigned int)STAT_TIME_NSEC( st, st_ctim ))
            changed |= CTIME_CHANGED;

    /* Check file user ID and group ID. */
    if (ce->st_uid != (unsigned int)st->st_uid ||
        ce->st_gid != (unsigned int)st->st_gid)
        changed |= OWNER_CHANGED;
    /* Check file mode. */
    if (ce->st_mode != (unsigned int)st->st_mode)
        changed |= MODE_CHANGED;
    #ifndef BGIT_WINDOWS
    /* Check device ID and file inode number. */
    if (ce->st_dev != (unsigned int)st->st_dev ||
        ce->st_ino != (unsigned int)st->st_ino)
        changed |= INODE_CHANGED;
    #endif
    /* Check file size. */
    if (ce->st_size != (unsigned int)st->st_size)
        changed |= DATA_CHANGED;
    return changed;
}
```

This is a straightforward function that makes use of if statements to compare the values of **cache_entry** structure members to those of the members of the **stat** structure of the working file corresponding to the cache entry. The bit flags that correspond to the different kinds of possible changes in these metadata are defined in lines 71 to 76:

```
71 #define MTIME_CHANGED   0x0001
72 #define CTIME_CHANGED   0x0002
73 #define OWNER_CHANGED   0x0004
74 #define MODE_CHANGED    0x0008
75 #define INODE_CHANGED   0x0010
76 #define DATA_CHANGED    0x0020
```

These hexadecimal numbers correspond to the decimal numbers

1, 2, 4, 8, 16, and 32 respectively. One can see in lines 99 to 122 that the composite value of the changed flag is obtained by performing a bitwise or with the relevant macro in lines 71 to 76.

13.3 show_differences

Synopsis

```
struct cache_entry *ce;
struct stat st;
unsigned long size;
char type[20];
void *new;
...
stat(ce->name, &st);
new = read_sha1_file(ce->sha1, type, &size);
show_differences(ce, &st, new, size);
```

Description

The **show_differences** function uses the **diff** shell command to display the differences between blob object data and the contents of the corresponding working file.

Function prototype

```
static void show_differences(struct cache_entry *ce, struct stat *cur,
                             void *old_contents, unsigned long long old_size);
```

Algorithm

The **show_differences** function first constructs the **diff** command by using the **snprintf** function, specifying the path of the file that is represented in the current cache entry. It then uses the **popen** function to create a pipe to the **diff** command and to return a pointer to the corresponding stream for writing. It then writes the blob object data to the command stream to complete the command, thus effectively executing the **diff** command.

Return value

The **show-differences** function has return type **void** and has no return value.

Code snippets

Here is the entirety of the short **show_differences** function:

```
static void show_differences(struct cache_entry *ce, struct stat *cur,
                             void *old_contents, unsigned long long old_size)
{
    static char cmd[1000];    /* String to store the diff command. */
    FILE *f;                  /* Declare a file pointer. */

    /*
     * Construct the diff command for this cache entry, which will be used to
     * display the differences between the blob data corresponding to the
     * cache entry and the contents of the corresponding working file.
     * Store the command string in `cmd`.
     */
    snprintf(cmd, sizeof(cmd), "diff --strip-trailing-cr -u - %s", ce->name);

    /*
     * Create a pipe to the diff command and return a pointer to the
     * corresponding stream for writing.
     */
    f = popen(cmd, "w");

    /*
     * Write the blob object data corresponding to the current cache entry to
     * the command stream to complete the command, thus effectively executing
     * the diff command.
     */
    fwrite(old_contents, old_size, 1, f);

    /* Close the command stream. */
    pclose(f);
```

```
167 }
```

Line 150 is where the `diff` shell command is constructed using the `snprintf` function. The `diff` shell command compares the contents of two text files line by line. In line 150, one of these files is the file represented in the current cache entry. The - symbol is a placeholder that indicates that the other set of contents to be used in the comparison will be coming from an input stream.

In line 156, a pipe to the `diff` command is created and a pointer to the corresponding stream is returned for writing. Line 163 writes the blob object data to this command stream to complete the `diff` command, thus effectively executing the command. Finally, the stream is closed in line 166.

Conclusion

We started this guidebook by stating our goals, which were twofold:

1. The first was to instruct the reader on the concepts and components that underlie Git's original repository and to provide a tutorial on the use of the original Git program.
2. The second was to provide an in-depth look at the C code of Git's original version.

Part 1 of this guidebook targeted the first goal and provided the reader with explanations of the concepts behind Git's initial version, how to install it, and how to use it.

Part 2 targeted the second goal and provided a detailed look at the more salient functions that are found in the 7 original Git commands.

By setting and working toward these dual goals, this guidebook provided views of the Git program from both a user perspective and a programmer perspective. Most readers who have already been using Git before reading this guidebook may only have had the former perspective, in which the gears that silently turn under the Git program remain hidden in an encasement.

In a manner of speaking, that box has been pried opened by curious minds, bearing a magnifier and light with enough lumens to make it possible to understand how the gears functioned. This being the case, the attentive reader will notice the absence of complexity. That is to say that, rather than being formidable, the code was found to be accessible. The functions used in Git's original version are available in C libraries to anyone who codes, or wishes to code, in the C language. The gears are familiar and mesh harmoniously.

But gears still need to be assembled by a skilled watchmaker to build a reliable timepiece. As apprentices, perhaps the most important benefit we could obtain from this guidebook is to take inspiration and techniques from the watchmaker's skills of assembling universally accessible parts into a robustly useful piece of craftsmanship. For, as apprentices, we might wish to build a useful tool as well.

Next Steps

Congrats! After reading this guidebook you now have an understanding of:

1. The basic concepts underlying Git's original repository
2. Installing the original Git program on your local machine
3. How to use and run Git's original 7 commands
4. The algorithms that underlie each of Git's original 7 commands / source files
5. C code extracts of the most important functions that power each of Git's original 7 commands
6. Exactly how Git's original C code works and implements Git's core concepts

If you're interested in learning more about Git and version control systems (VCS) in general, we have many resources and articles available on our **website initialcommit.com** and **Git blog**. Covered areas include a wide range of topics such as:

- **Overviews & usage of every Git command**
- **Git guides & tutorials**
- **Advanced Git & version control systems (VCS)**
- **Git general knowledge**

We also created a custom command-line tool called **Git-Story** for creating video animations (.mp4) of your commit history directly from your Git repo. Consider trying it out if you're a more visual learner!

Thanks so much for reading and if you have any general questions about Git or this guidebook feel free to reach out to me any time at this email address:

jacob@initialcommit.io

Wishing you all the best in achieving your software development goals,
Jacob (Jack) Stopak, Initial Commit LLC
initialcommit.com

Appendix

A.1 Installing MSYS2 and MinGW-w64 on Windows

Here we provide the steps for installing the MSYS2 and MinGW-w64 environment in Windows systems.

Download and install MSYS2

Depending on your Windows system, download the 32-bit or 64-bit MSYS2 installer from this website:

http://www.msys2.org

Follow the instructions given in the website to install MSYS2, including the part about updating the packages.

Launch an MSYS2 terminal

After installation, launch an MSYS2 terminal. To do this, look for the MSYS2 32bit or MSYS2 64bit folder in the Start menu. Under this folder, click on MSYS2 MinGW 32-bit or MSYS2 MinGW 64-bit, again depending on your system. This should open an MSYS2 terminal.

Note that when you open an MSYS2 terminal, you will land in your MSYS2 home directory. As far as MSYS2 is concerned, this directory is:

```
/home/your_username
```

where `your_username` is your actual Windows username. The `cd` and `pwd` commands are useful for navigating the MSYS2 directories. The `cd` command without an argument takes you back to your home directory, and the `pwd` command displays the present working directory:

```
$ cd
$ pwd
```

The actual Windows path of this directory is the following for a 64-bit and 32-bit system respectively:

```
C:\msys64\home\your_username
```

```
C:\msys32\home\your_username
```

When you install the original Git program, you will need to download and extract the archive in this directory. Please see section 3.2, **Installation steps**, in Chapter 3 for instructions on installing the original Git program.

Create a bin directory

Create a `bin` directory in your MSYS2 home directory, i.e., create a `/home/your_username/bin` directory. This directory is where you will install the 7 original Git commands. By installing the commands in this directory, the original Git commands can be executed from any directory below your MSYS2 home directory.

To create the `bin` directory, type the following commands:

```
$ cd
$ mkdir bin
```

Add the bin directory to PATH

Next, you need to add the path to your `bin` directory to the `PATH` environment variable so that it will be included in the command search path. You can set the value of `PATH` in the `.profile` file in your home directory by typing the following commands:

```
$ cd
$ echo 'PATH="$HOME/bin:$PATH"' >> .profile
```

And then execute the commands in the `.profile` file:

```
$ source .profile
```

To check that your home `bin` directory has been added to the `PATH` environment variable, type the following command:

```
$ echo $PATH
```

You should see the path to your home `bin` directory at the beginning of the string that is displayed.

Install development packages

Install the base development package and the MinGW-w64 toolchain. For 64-bit systems, type the following command on the terminal:

```
$ pacman -S --needed base-devel mingw-w64-x86_64-toolchain
```

For 32-bit systems, use the following command:

```
$ pacman -S --needed base-devel mingw-w64-i686-toolchain
```

Install the zlib development package

The zlib development package will be needed by the original Git program to deflate and inflate data. Type the following command to install it in the MSYS2 environment:

```
$ pacman -S zlib-devel
```

Install the OpenSSL development package

The OpenSSL development package will be needed by the original Git program to calculate SHA-1 hash values. Type the following command to install it in the MSYS2 environment:

```
$ pacman -S openssl-devel
```

Once you have successfully completed the steps given above, you are ready to install the original Git program. The steps are the same as those given in section 3.2, "Installation steps," in Chapter 3.

Made in United States
Orlando, FL
04 November 2026

90206124R00079